THE GIRLFRIEND'S GUIDE TO RETIREMENT

NFB
Buffalo, New York

THE GIRLFRIEND'S GUIDE TO RETIREMENT

By
Susan L. Klute

Copyright © 2024 Susan L. Klute

Printed in the United States of America

The Girlfriend's Guide to Retirement/ Klute 1st Edition

ISBN: 978-1-953610-59-1

Nonfiction> Stages of Life> Retirement
Nonfiction> Self-Help>Empowerment
Nonfiction> Later Stages of Life Planning
Nonfiction> Inspirational
Nonfiction> Female Author

No part of this book may be reproduced or transmitted in any form by any means, electronic or mechanical, including photocopying, recording, or by any information storage and retrieval system without permission in writing by the author.

NFB Publishing
119 Dorchester Road
Buffalo, New York 14213
For more information visit Nfbpublishing.com

This book is dedicated to all the amazing women who are ready to think about and plan for an exciting and fulfilling chapter in their lives. I applaud you for being proactive and intentional to ensure it gives you joy and contentment at the same time. I send my love and best wishes to each of you.

Contents

Introduction	9
Part 1	
Chaspter 1: Travel	21
Chapter 2: Projects	29
Chapter 3: Tasks	35
Chapter 4: Reading Lists	43
Chapter 5: Exercise	51
Chapter 6: Give Back	57
Chapter 7: Learn New Things (Hobbies)	63
Summary	71
Part 2	
Chapter 8: No One is Perfect and Neither Are You	75
Chapter 9: Self-Care	79
Chapter 10: Take Care of Your Body	85
Chapter 11: If Something is Broke, Fix It	93
Chapter 12: Enjoy Your Family	103
Chapter 13: Stay Connected to Your Friends And Make New Ones	109
Chapter 14: Don't Let Yourself Go	115
Chapter 15: Do Your Best to Get Rid of Bad Habits	121
Chapter 16: Drink Tons of Water	131
Chapter 17: Have Fun!	137
Chapter 18: Laugh Daily!	141
Chapter 19: You Can Still Feel Joy!	145
Chapter 20: Never Stop Learning or Exploring	149
Chapter 21: Embrace Your Never-Ending Vacation	153
Chapter 22: Surround Yourself With Things You Love	157
Chapter 23: Rescue a Dog or Cat	161
Chapter 24: Have Faith in Your Life	165
Challenge	171

Introduction

So you're thinking about retirement?

Retirement is different for everyone. Some people think about it during their entire career. Some people never retire. There is no standard retirement age any longer. You could be 40, 90 or anything in between. Me? I didn't think about it seriously until I was in my 60's. I loved working. I started my full-time career as a church secretary and ended it in learning and development. Most of my career was spent in sales and management, and boy, was it fun and lucrative. But after I turned 60, my mindset (and my body) began to change. Work felt harder and more stressful but I still enjoyed it. Then one day, I didn't. I was 64 and thought, I think I'm done. Everyone's journey is different and you will know when you are ready.

At first, I thought I would work until the end of the year after my 65th birthday but my kids thought I was crazy. We live in Western New York. Why would you want to retire in the winter? I gave them the "yes, but I won't be 65 until October" excuse. So what? We think you should consider retiring at the beginning of summer instead. I decided to explore my options and low and behold, I was able to pull it off.

I decided to list all the things that I might jump into when I retire so I could start putting my wish list together. I gave a three month notice to my boss to give her plenty of time to look for my replacement and then I began dreaming about the "Summer of Susan". It was so exciting! I felt like a kid the week before summer vacation. I also decided to keep a diary of my life for the first year of retirement and the lessons I learned along the way. I hoped to someday pass along these learnings to others so they might know what it could be like for them in their future. People that are still working ask me what I do all day. Keep reading if you'd like to know the answer.

I have added questions along the way for you to ponder. I hope you will take the time to really think them through. You can answer with your initial thoughts as you read through this book or wait until the end. You may want to answer and then go back after you've thought about it. However you do it, you will want to get a journal or some other way to record your answers. This will be your initial plan for your retirement filled with your dreams and goals for the future. This is your journey. Enjoy it in the manner that makes you feel the most comfortable.

So, buckle up and learn what you have in store for you should you decide it's time to call it quits from your career. It really can come at any time if you play your cards (and your money) right but my first bit of advice is don't wait too long. I was adamant about enjoying my time while my body and mind were still fit and you should, too. I am not a doctor and these learnings are entirely from my experience so take them or leave them; it's your choice. I hope you get to enjoy every day of your life from here on out whether you are working or not.

So, have you thought about retirement? If so, when did those thoughts emerge? What made you start to think about it? What is "your goal age" to retire from your full-time career?

Prepare for this huge life change, mentally and physically

There are steps to take before you inform your boss that you are ready to take this huge leap in your career or should I say out of your career. The first thing you should do is talk to your partner if you are lucky enough to have one. This decision will affect their life, too. My husband was already retired and settled into his own routine. When I dropped the bomb on him, he was nervous about it. He really wanted me to work until the end of the year and if I'm being honest with myself, I think he would have been happy if I just kept going. So, did I cave? No. I shared my feelings openly with him and he understood how passionate I was about my end date. We both agreed that it was time.

Robin, my husband and I have had a financial consultant for years so I reached out to him next to ensure I was financially ready. We discussed my 401K and Roth accounts and he mapped out my plan for the next twenty years barring any big health or financial disasters out of our control. He felt confident that I had enough money in my accounts and savings to retire comfortably. This is the biggest hurdle for everyone. It's not too early to begin these discussions with a financial analyst even if retirement is years away. The more time you take to plan financially, the more comfortable you will feel once you finally make your decision on a date. If you don't have a financial consultant, ask your family and friends to see who they might be working with. You may be able to search online but with something this important, it would be optimal to find one that someone you trust is already working with.

I spoke to our HR department to understand what my options were for medical coverage should I leave the company before I turned 65. HR educated me on my Cobra options. Cobra is expensive so I was hoping I wouldn't have to use it but if I did, it was there. If you are over 65, then you will be eligible for Medicare so this will not be a consideration for you.

I met with a Medicare consultant to research what the options were for myself and Robin going forward. She gave us her recommendations for the interim period and beyond. I would go two months without medical insurance and if an emergency did come up, I had a 63-day lookback period where I could get Cobra coverage if I needed it. If not, she felt it was a waste of money. She would sign Robin up for his part b (Medicare Advantage) effective August 1 and provided me with the forms necessary from my HR department for Medicare. She would sign me up for Medicare and my part b (Medicare Advantage) effective October 1. My 65th birthday was October 31 but you are eligible on the first day of your birth month. You may have different medical coverage so check with your company on how to proceed. Be sure to keep your Medicare Consultant's phone number handy because they will be invaluable to you in the future when it comes to keeping your coverage effective and especially when you are looking for new medical providers that are in your network. More about that later. You can again ask family and friends for a recommendation but if no one can provide one, you can find one in your area on this link: Independent Medicare Agents Near Me - free online directory (medicaresupp.org). You just put your zip code in and the agents close to you will pop up. These consultants are free to you and are compensated by the Medicare insurance companies, all of them, not just one so they are neutral when helping you choose the right coverage for you. In your initial meeting, they will ask you for the names of all your current providers to ensure they are in network for the company you choose. Their job is to ensure that you get the best coverage and understanding of the programs that each insurance company provides. You will have many to choose from and they are all the same price so it really is all about which one you are most comfortable with. Each year you will have the opportunity to change insurance companies through open enrollment, just like when you were working so if you find that you are not happy with your first choice, you can meet with your consultant again the following year and go through the process again. If you want to keep the same insurance company, you do not have to do anything during open enrollment. Your coverage will continue. There is a standard premium for Medical Advantage of $162.90 per person. If you are collecting Social Security, it will come out of your monthly check. If you are not collecting yet, you will receive a bill in the mail. If you have continued health insurance coverage from your company, then you will not require Medicare Advantage coverage but you will still be required to apply for Medicare. Everyone 65 years of age should apply for the program and it is free.

Once I had all my ducks in a row and the confidence that I was ready to make this move, I put in my three-month notice. I worked with my boss on the plan to begin moving my work, interviewing and training my replacement and ultimately saying my good bye's. It felt so strange but also freeing! I was so fortunate to retire from a company that I loved and I received so much love on my way out. The leadership announced my departure on an "all company meeting" via Zoom and did a beautiful presentation on the impact I had on the organization. So many people reached out afterwards with personal farewells. The company even gave me a lovely parting gift. Since I was a remote worker, the other local folks also took me out to dinner and gave me a journal to send me on my way. It was filled with personal messages from my co-workers and I was awed as I read it. Don't underestimate the impact that you have had on others and take it all in. I hope you all get to retire with love and fond farewells, too.

Before you leave, be sure to save any personal items you may have on your work computer. Your company may have extraction prevention to protect their data so you don't steal anything "work related". I know you won't since you are done, right? What I'm talking about are passwords you may have saved in an Excel document for personal accounts or Christmas letters you may have written in the past. If you used your work email for personal websites, change them. All these actions should be done either before or right after you give your notice. You will discover there are probably no other documents that you will require in your new life. It surprised me how much I didn't miss that computer that I had been glued to for my career. If you believe you will want to use a computer in your retirement, now is the time to buy a new one. I chose a laptop that was made by the same company as my work computer so that I was familiar with it. I loaded my personal email on it and I bought a Microsoft "lifetime" license for Office. I sent my corporate equipment back to my employer and converted my home office to my personal office. I even cleaned out my filing cabinet of anything work related and shredded it. And yes, I recycled my awards and replaced them with personal items. I disconnected my headset and camera and still haven't reconnected them to my new laptop a year later. It's funny how your mindset changes so quickly when you are ready. If you don't want or need a home office, repurpose the room or space into something fun for the future. Open your mind to new possibilities; they are everywhere!

Robin asked me if I wanted to have another party with our friends and family that he was happy to throw for me, but I declined. I'm not comfortable with big gatherings and said I was thrilled with what I had already received from my company. Some of my close friends did want to celebrate this milestone with me with intimate events that we planned together like a live theater show and dinner and even foot massages and dinner. I loved them all. They meant so much to me and I was so grateful for the outpouring of love from each of them. That was me. You should decide what is best for you. You may love a big party or you may want to go quietly. This is your choice and it is all about you.

Now you are ready for the next chapter of your life: one where you are in charge of your time, your activities and your adventures. Be prepared mentally for your final week and plan some personal good byes to ease yourself out. Plan something very special for the first days of your retirement. Don't just sit in a chair and say, oh well, now I can do nothing. Take time away from your regular life, if possible, to think, meditate, challenge yourself to do things you don't normally do, talk to people outside your circle, share openly, be honest with yourself and open your heart and mind to new possibilities. Don't judge yourself or others. We are all amazing and unique in our own way.

Preparation Checklist:

1. Have an honest discussion with your partner if you have one to let them know of your intentions. Remember, share your feelings openly and listen to their responses. Don't let them talk you out of retiring if that is your true desire.

2. Talk to your financial consultant if you have one. If you don't, consider finding one by reaching out to others you know and trust to ask for recommendations.

3. Talk to your HR rep to understand your options for medical coverage once you retire and make arrangements if necessary to replace what you had. If you are not yet 65 you may need to purchase private insurance.

4. Meet with a Medicare consultant. This is a free service. Ask for recommendations from your HR rep or a friend who lives in your area. You will require someone who lives in your state. If these are not options, you can look one up on [Independent Medicare Agents Near Me - free online directory (medicaresupp.org)](https://medicaresupp.org). You just put your zip code in and the agents close to you will pop up.

5. Talk to your immediate supervisor and give your notice. I gave mine three months because of my position. Don't wait until two weeks before your final day unless that is the standard procedure with your company. Your manager can guide you but give them the opportunity to celebrate you.

6. If you have used a computer in your job, remove any personal items on it.

7. Delete the ones you no longer want and transfer the ones you wish to keep.

8. If you don't have a personal computer at home, buy one.

9. Change your email address on any websites you will continue to use from a work email to a personal email.

10. Take these actions as soon as you put your notice in.

11. Discuss what type of celebration you would like to have with your loved ones. Be honest about what you are comfortable with. Write your ideas here:

12. Plan something special for yourself for your last day or the following week. It can be something as simple as going out for a nice dinner or a dream trip. Make it your own. It's important to change your mindset as you go from a very structured life to a flexible one.

Part I

When I first retired, I made a list on my old whiteboard that I used in my job of all the different categories that I thought I should focus on going forward. I updated the items under each of them as the year progressed, (at least most of the time – LOL). I hope this guide will inspire you on your retirement journey.

Chapter One

Travel

Travel is the #1 goal of most people when they retire. I remember while I was working, whenever I encountered someone who was in the latter part of their career, when they talked about their retirement goals, it was all about travel. I have had a wonderful career where travel was part of it so I have seen many other states and countries during my years of work. I also had a career in sales and won many trips to take with my husband throughout the years. Growing up, my mom feared flying so as a child, we didn't take luxurious trips abroad or even long road trips. When I became an adult, I wanted my family to see more than I did. Unfortunately, we didn't have enough money to fly so we did road trips instead, not luxurious but well intentioned and fun with the budget we had. The reason I share this with you is because travel was not my #1 priority but definitely on my list of things I wanted to do in retirement. I strived to figure out how to see as much of the world as I could, using my time and money wisely to see and enjoy the places I would most like to go.

One thing to keep in mind is that your time is limited. Although I am in excellent health for my age, I do not have the physical strength and stamina that I had in my 30's. Am I normal? I would say that I am average. There will be those of you who are in better shape, physically and monetarily and those of you who are not so fortunate. Make your plans according to your desires and your "limitations". Oh, and if you have pets, don't forget to line up a reliable house sitter or somewhere to board them. You don't want to worry about your babies while you're gone.

In my first year of retirement, I took a variety of trips with a variety of people. On my last "official" day of work, I left for a retreat at a wonderful center for yoga and health called Kripalu (Homepage | Kripalu) in the Berkshires in Massachusetts with my daughter, Jessie. This was intentional. Jessie had suggested that it might help me transition from full time work to full time fun. Months before I retired, she sent me information on a retreat called "The Art and Science of Rest" and boy, did that resonate with me. Who wouldn't love a retreat like that after hanging up a 47-year career? Sign me up! She took a different track which gave me the opportunity to be myself and share openly with a group of people I didn't know and would probably never see again. This experience was four days of formal sessions and activities like yoga, both within my track and outside of it along with free time to explore the grounds and enjoy delicious healthy food and casual conversations with other folks at the venue. When I say it exceeded my expectations by a million, I am not exaggerating. What I loved the most about it, was that my group was filled with other "high achievers". I got to hear about their struggles and quite honestly, about some of the mistakes they had made in their lives and even in their retirement. They celebrated my announcement that I had literally just retired that first day and the calm that began to overtake me as each day unfolded was most needed and quite magical. The planned activities each affected me differently, some calming and others so thought provoking that I continued to ruminate on them even after I returned home. The accommodations were modest so the trip expenses were also modest. Getting to spend those four days with my daughter in between our sessions was priceless. I think this is my #1 recommendation as far as travel goes: plan something right away to help you calm your mind, put your career behind you and think about what retirement might really mean to you so you can think about your future.

The next trip I took was with my husband, Robin. This was just an overnighter. How many times have you had friends and/or family invite you to come and visit them? How many times have you said yes and gone? When you are working, spontaneity is tough. A friend of mine has a lake house two plus hours away from our home. In a conversation with her, she mentioned that Robin and I should come out for a Saturday visit now that I am retired. She is still working so weekends are when she is there with her husband. I let her know that I would love to do that and we set a date on the spot. I think that's the key. I didn't want to impose by staying overnight with them so instead, I booked a nearby motel so we could drive home the next day. The whole experience was lovely. They excitedly showed us around their new property and we enjoyed a day of snacks and wine on the porch, a boat ride around the lake and a yummy dinner before heading to our motel. She and her husband are so proud of this dream come true and beamed while sharing it with us. I took in their love and excitement and felt so grateful for the generous invitation as well as their friendship. And Robin and I got to explore the nearby town after a good night's sleep and breakfast the next day before heading home. Travel doesn't have to be exotic, long or glamorous to be meaningful. Enjoy the ability to be spontaneous.

I wanted to plan time away in my "First summer of Susan" but my mind was boggled by retiring earlier in the year and it was already July so I kept it simple. I have always had a hankering to go back to the Thousand Islands which is only a four-hour drive from our home. I had been there thirty-five years ago but Robin had never been. I asked him to check out options on Airbnb of cottages for a five-day rental. He found one that looked quite quaint and I asked him to book it. The drive was easy and our hosts for the house were wonderful. We took a tour of the islands and Boldt Castle. We made delicious breakfasts each day and walked down to the dock to sit and enjoy the water and the wildlife. We dined at different restaurants each evening while exploring different areas. We had a fire one evening. I hiked and explored the area around our cottage. It was relaxing and I enjoyed spending time with Robin without distractions from work, our pets, our kids and even our house. Are there any areas that you may have enjoyed in the past that your partner may not? Share it with them. Explore how those areas may have changed or may be exactly the same. You never know and that's the fun of it. If your partner isn't interested in going on that hike with you, go alone. Just be safe. Bring your phone and obviously, don't go anywhere dangerous, even if your partner is with you.

Next it was time for another retreat, "Reconnect to your Wholeness" with my daughter, Danielle. This one was done by a friend of hers and De really wanted to go and invited me to accompany her. This experience was at a retreat center only about an hour away from De's house so an easy drive. It was more expensive than my other retreat but again, sharing it with my daughter was priceless. The content was interesting and I loved the intimacy of the activities since there were only four of us along with the two facilitators. I came away with knowledge and a love for those other women, nature and gratitude for my daughter's desire to spend that time with me. Whenever you get the opportunity to do something for yourself and more importantly for one of your children, if you are lucky enough to have them, say yes. Do you think it's overly expensive? Not sure you're going to love it? Don't let your doubts get in the way. Just go for it! This was only three days but it touched me deeply.

Okay, you're probably thinking, aren't you going to do anything big? Don't you want to take that dream trip? Of course, I did but you can't just take one dream trip after another. I got really lucky on my first year of retirement because my niece, Zoe got married. So what Susan, we get wedding invitations all the time. Really? Are they in Nice, France? That's right! We got the "Save the Date" in plenty of time to plan this amazing vacation. My children really did it up by spending weeks in France, going to Paris and experiencing as much as they could. I knew in my heart that Robin would not be able to do a marathon so our trip was much more modest. I planned for a week in Nice only. I booked our flights out of Toronto which is a two-hour drive from our home and that's with ideal situations since the bridge crossing from the U.S. to Canada can become a burden (it wasn't, thank goodness). We stayed in one of the recommended hotels, adding the beach package. We had never been to France so Nice was enough for me because of Robin's limitations. Our daughters joined us when we got there and that was so fortunate. My brother, Bob and sister-in-law, Elaine were also there so we got to spend time with them before the wedding activities got into full swing. This week away brought me and my brother back together after many years of busy careers and families. I felt our love rekindle and it warmed my heart. The wedding, the welcome dinner the night before and the beach day the day after left us all speechless. Everything could not have been lovelier especially the bride. Robin struggled with the walking and chose to stay behind at the hotel on some occasions. Having the girls and others to count on made the trip perfect for me. If they had not been there, I would have struggled with just Robin. I love my husband but his limitations keep him from accompanying me on physical adventures. I love the water and spent the afternoons in the Mediterranean with De, Rich (De's husband) and Jessie, not Robin. I explored Nice with the kids as well, not Robin. Robin and I did take a tour of the French Riviera and Monaco after the kids left and it was tough for him. I found seating at every stop for Robin to sit and rest while I explored and walked on my own. It broke my heart. I think it showed us both where we currently are with our physical capabilities and desires. This is why it's so important to take the trips you most desire as soon as you can. If you can do it while you are young, do it. Don't wait until you retire to take those dream trips. You may not be able to.

So, those were the trips I took in my first year of retirement. All of them were different and I learned so many things along the way. My biggest takeaway is to keep an open mind. For those of you who are married, you may not be able to keep your partner as your traveling companion for all your trips. Have honest conversations. Tailor your travel to you and your capabilities. I have already booked a bus tour of New England in the fall. While I have been to Massachusetts, New Hampshire and Connecticut, I have always wanted to go to all the states in New England to see the foliage. I researched the tour with the company before I booked it to understand how much walking there would be and what the accommodations would be like for someone who struggles with walking. I discussed it with Robin before locking it down. He felt he could do it. I let him know that this trip will be a good indicator for the future. If he truly can't "keep up", then I would like to travel with others who can. I know, it sounds mean. How can you leave your husband behind? Well, I worked for 47 years and I have worked hard to stay fit and strong my whole life. Robin worked hard, too but once he stopped working, he chose to sit instead. That was his choice and I have respected it for nine years. Unfortunately, his lifestyle has also affected his body and his refusal to seek medical assistance has also kept him from getting better. Again, that is his choice but it is not my burden to carry. If he chooses not to fight for physical strength, then I will travel with others, my kids or a girlfriend. This is not an easy decision but it is a necessary one for me. It may not be for you. We are all different but I am choosing to enjoy my retirement and my travel dreams for as long as I can. I hope you do, too. Don't wait.

1. Think about the trips you would like to take and list them here. Prioritize by desire, difficulty and cost. Who will be traveling with you? List your initial thoughts and then start planning. Don't forget about a special trip to take right after you retire if you believe it might help with your transition.

Notes:

Chapter Two

Projects

I had many projects during the year but cleaning was not at the top of my list. I've heard from so many women that when they quit working, whether it's a job loss or retirement, the first thing they do is clean everything. While I was passionate about cleaning out certain things (like my basement), it was not top of mind for me. Instead, I tackled projects as the motivation hit me and I learned very quickly that I couldn't go for hours and hours like when I was young. I took projects in increments and when I was tired, I quit.

My top priority for the year was writing this book. I wanted to prove to myself that I could do it since I've always had a passion for writing and I was looking for a vehicle to sort out my feelings throughout the adventure. It was very effective. I kept a journal throughout the year, "typing" almost daily with the theme for the day, what I did, how I felt throughout my day and a lesson I learned. What I found was that my routines changed throughout the year: my activities, my desires, pretty much everything.

One thing that I valued right from the beginning was my mornings. I no longer had to get up early, get ready for work and either run out of the door to drive to an office or get up to my home office and put my "work face" on. So, what did I want my mornings to look like instead of the race to work? Since my retirement began on July 1, I got up, put the kettle on and fed the animals (dogs and cat, not farm). I took my tea out to the porch, put my feet up and began my day enjoying the birds and nature that I was surrounded by. I have lived in my house for 19 years and now I can enjoy the beauty that I have worked so hard to achieve. I jump start my brain by doing Wordle first and shared my success (or not) with my daughter, Danielle since she also partook in that activity. It was a lovely way to say good morning to her. Then I would read my personal email which was filled with messages I **wanted** to read, trivia, inspiration, sales from my favorite stores, travel deals, etc. Next, I checked out Instagram and then my notifications on Facebook. I didn't want to miss anyone's birthday. I also took the time to put thoughtful comments on posts that really meant something to me. I read the local newspaper which I still get daily and the mail depending on when they both arrived. I am very "agenda driven" so I cut myself off after three cups of tea, having breakfast after my second cup. It felt like I was on vacation at first and I guess I am, a permanent one of my choosing. I felt my stress level begin to sink slowly with each passing day. Now that you are retired, it's time for you to revise your morning routine, too. Don't forget some of the basics like rehydrating when you first wake up before tea or coffee. I drink a 12 oz. glass of water upon rising followed by a glass of celery juice. I also stretch my body to get all the stiffness from sleeping out. Would a walk in your neighborhood feel right for you or are you ready to head to the gym or the "Y" for a workout. Maybe a nice meditation or prayer to set your mind for a positive day. Everyone is different so start with "what you've always wanted to do" if you had the time. If you don't like it, change it. There are no rules anymore.

Some of the other projects I did complete were cleaning out certain areas of my home. Since I still have a house cleaner, I had the luxury of choosing things Molly didn't clean and doing them myself, like the basement, the barn and generally purging things that I no longer wanted or needed. One of the toughest ones I am still dealing with is my closet and my clothes in general. Boy, has my wardrobe changed! Who needs all those dresses, suit coats and formal dresses anymore? I kept my favorites but those formal dresses are hard to part with because of the cost and the memories. The mother of the bride dresses may linger forever. When it comes to your business clothes, it might feel easier if you could donate them to a local charity that help women get back into the workforce. For formal clothes, your local high school may enjoy them for future plays. Or just donating them to a local church, shelter, Salvation Army, etc. will assure you that they will go to someone who will appreciate them as much as you did. Thank them for serving you well and wish them a good life.

I did projects around the house that were fun, too, like a wall mural. That one started as a couple of decals because I didn't want to paint the whole hallway because of a hole and a few dings and turned into a full-blown bird community. It probably sounds silly to young people but doing big home projects become so much harder as you get older. I would love to get new carpeting in said hallway along with one of the bedrooms but having to move all the furniture and repainting everything seems so big; therefore, my wall mural and a couple of throw rugs were the answer for now. This area is my "guest wing" which is mostly used by my grandchildren so perfection in the decorating is not required since they made most of those lovely stains on my rug anyway. They still love it and I don't feel the pressure of keeping it pristine.

Gardening is also one of my big projects. We hired a landscaper in my last year of work which was a dream of mine. I always wanted to have a "fresh start" from a professional and I invested in it. Since I am that daily porch sitter until the snow flies, this was really important to me. It may not be for you. Not only did they redo my huge garden beds, they also put in a patio off my porch and walkways and granite steps in three different areas and did hardscaping around our hot tub. Again, I feel like I'm on vacation everyday enjoying the beauty of my own property. I think that's the whole purpose of projects, don't you? So that you are in your happy place in your home. Now, I spend my time maintaining and adding to these beautiful areas. The bees and butterflies love them, too.

I think it's important for you to spend your time and your money on projects that are important to you and your partner, again if you have one. What have you been wanting to do for years? You may not want to add anything else to your current home and instead, move to a new situation. Are the stairs too much? Is the house too big? Or maybe you are just ready for a change. Whatever your motivation is, just do it. I am so grateful that our mortgage is paid and we no longer have that monthly expense. Am I ready to move? Not quite yet but you never know what will make me change my mind. Moving is another tremendous undertaking, so unless you really want to find another residence, I would table it until you have a solid reason to go. I have a friend who wanted to take it on the road and rather than store all their belongings, sold their house with everything included. Not a bad idea really. Or take your personal items and have that estate sale now instead of waiting until you're gone. There really are endless options.

So, do you have a book inside you that is ready to be written? It can be as simple as poetry, your life story to leave for your family, inspiration from your own life learnings or maybe the next great novel. I love mysteries but think about what's in your heart.

Maybe you are ready to share your knowledge through a podcast, You Tube video or even writing articles for your local newspaper. The possibilities are endless. Meditate about the projects that might get you excited. Whatever you take on, you don't have to be perfect. You can always hire a professional to bring your dream to life if you have the budget or maybe you can learn a new skill through your local college or adult education. I'll talk more about that when we get to hobbies and learning new things. Whatever project you take on, big or small, prepare before you start. Don't get frustrated. If you get stuck, ask for help. You've got all the time in the world to get it done.

So what projects would you like to put on your "to do" list? Start listing them here and put a star next to the ones that are most important to you. When you are ready to tackle one, list out what supplies you might require and assistance if necessary. Don't forget to educate yourself first if it's something you've never done. Do you require a budget? Don't forget to get estimates if it's a big one.

-
-
-
-
-
-
-
-
-
-
-
-
-
-

Notes:

Chapter Three

Tasks

You may wonder what the difference is between projects and tasks. Me too. I kept a list of tasks, smaller jobs on my board to get them out of my head. I have found in retirement that there are very few deadlines and our time is "unlimited". With that being said, when I thought of something that I wanted to do, I didn't necessarily stop everything and do it but I wanted to remember it for another day. Did I always get to everything on my list? Absolutely not but really....how important is it?

The other activities that fell under tasks for me were chores that my husband may have owned while we were working that I wanted to either take over or at least learn about. I started with the laundry. This chore has been owned by Robin for our whole married life. When we got engaged we discussed how we might "divide and conquer" since we were both working full time. The big ones were these: laundry and cooking went to Robin and cleaning and grocery shopping were mine. There were other smaller ones that naturally got divided but it was so important to me not to have to do everything. It worked very well for us. With that being said, I was satisfied with Robin's results with the laundry over the years but now that I was retired, I had a desire to take it over. Why? Because I wanted to control how my clothes were cared for. I loved folding them for maximum wrinkle prevention and putting my things away after each load instead of sorting through the piles that Robin left me in a laundry basket throughout the years. I also had to learn how to use our washer and dryer at age 64. Funny, right? Now that I have been retired for a year, I have incorporated his help again in moving the laundry along if I have a busy day, but I enjoy the process of doing it regularly.

Another task that I wanted to take back on a more regular basis was cooking. Robin is a great cook but he cooks the things he likes consistently. He loves sausage, cheeseburgers and spaghetti followed up by a pot of goulash from the leftover sauce. I was interested in incorporating more fish, chicken and fun and healthy dishes overall. Do I cook every night now? No. I love the flexibility of sharing this responsibility. When I see a recipe online that intrigues me, I volunteer to cook that evening. Or if I just want something in particular, I call "it". Sometimes we'll share the cooking; Robin might be grilling while I'm preparing the sides. Generally, whoever cooks gives the joy of doing the dishes to the other one. I also like doing the dishes so that the kitchen is clean and clear when I'm done. We have a dishwasher so it's really no big deal. I hope you do, too. I am a great cook and I enjoy benefitting from my skill. Robin and I don't go out for dinner very much anymore for a few reasons. We used to go out while I was working remotely to get me out of the house a couple times during the week. That is no longer necessary. The cost is also prohibitive at this point in our lives, especially when we are disappointed in a meal. Why get gussied up for the inconvenience of going out to eat just to eat? We like to save that expense for special occasions with friends and family which means we still go out an average of once a week. Are you the type that enjoys going out for your main meal every day? Then do it! This is your time to enjoy the things that mean the most to you.

I have found that I enjoy a standard healthy (for the most part) breakfast daily. I attended a women's breakfast at church and tasted a "Baked Oatmeal" and I loved it. The cook was kind enough to give me the recipe and I now make it consistently. Here's the recipe if you'd like to try it:

Overnight Blueberry Baked Oatmeal

- 2 cups old fashioned rolled oats
- 2 cups unsweetened almond milk or regular milk
- 1/3 cup pure maple syrup or regular syrup
- 2 tsp ground cinnamon

Mix the above in a bowl, cover and refrigerate over-night. The next morning add and mix together:

- 1 large beaten egg
- 1 teaspoon baking powder

Then add 1 ½ cups blueberries (fresh or thawed frozen). I don't eat fruit during the day so I have increased this to 2 cups of fruit and this is where you can get creative. Any kind of berry will work or pitted cherries, apples, pears, raisins, whatever you have on hand. Pour into a greased 8 x 8 baking pan.

Streusel Topping:

- 1 cup old fashioned oats
- ½ cup flour
- ½ cup brown sugar
- ¼ teaspoon salt
- ½ cup melted butter

Mix the dry ingredients together and pour the melted butter into them. Sprinkle this over the top of the soaked oatmeal. Options: sprinkle nuts (pecans or walnuts) on top of the streusel along with a few mini white chocolate chips. Bake for 30 – 40 minutes at 375 degrees until most of the liquid is absorbed. Let it cool for at least 10 minutes and cut it into 9 equal squares. Store it in the refrigerator and enjoy. It even makes a good evening snack!

THE GIRLFRIEND'S GUIDE TO RETIREMENT

For lunch, I love soup. I make a pot regularly and since I have it every day, I keep it fresh by using different meats, vegetables, bases and spices. I don't often use pastas because of the calories but I will once in a while. The easiest thing to do is to put your basic ingredients in the search bar of your computer browser and add soup recipes. The possibilities are almost endless. I look for recipes that have four or five stars and see what I have. You can substitute vegetables for what you have on hand and if I don't have a spice or other ingredient, I will "ask Alexa" what I can substitute or you can look it up on your computer. If I find a recipe I love, I save it in my favorites so I can make it again in the future. I use this method for dinners, too. I do still have cookbooks which I will refer to sometimes but with the internet, it feels so much easier. If you are new to cooking, you can even find You Tube videos with step-by-step instructions. I always tell my children, if you can read, you can cook and bake. When starting out, stay as close to the recipe as you can but as you get more and more comfortable, you will find yourself getting creative and going more by feel and taste. Don't be afraid to try something new!

Paying our bills was also Robin's responsibility over the years. I honestly had no idea what they were, how he paid them or even how much money we had. This practice can really get a couple in trouble but this is an area where Robin shone. When we were young and money was extremely tight, he was a master at knowing which bills to pay and when. He managed our money like a financial genius. Now we are fortunate to have enough money to pay our bills comfortably. I thought about taking over the process but he really enjoys doing it so we've kept it with him. Here is my message around this task: even if you don't own it, understand it! Know how to access your banks and your accounts. Are you getting bills in the mail or do you pay them online with an email reminder going to your partner? How many of your bills get automatically deducted from your account? You should know exactly what this process is so that if anything happens to your partner, you can easily take over and vice versa. It's critical to know any passwords that are on your online accounts. Keep a list somewhere safe. Having your bank accounts and bill pay online will streamline this process. No more having to plan ahead to mail a check. If you have accounts with only one of your names on it, add the missing one. This is the time to think about what might happen if one of you becomes incapacitated and the other has to take over. Knowing your financial status is key to a happy retirement.

Speaking of the possibility of something happening to your partner, do you have a will? How about a healthcare proxy and power of attorney? You should both be prepared should anything happen to either of you or both. Robin and I had none of these things before we retired which is even worse for us since we are a blended family. You will want your estate to be divided according to your desires. Discuss your wishes before you meet with an attorney so there are no surprises. If you don't have an attorney, there are "Elder Lawyers" available that will charge a set fee for all of the necessary paperwork mentioned above. We paid $825 for everything so don't let cost prohibit you from doing this very necessary task. If you don't already have one, you can find them online by typing in "elder lawyers in my area" to see who can help you.

There are so many tasks that you have probably shared as you were working and now is the time to do what you enjoy. DON'T TAKE EVERYTHING BACK! Just because you retired, doesn't mean it's time to take care of your partner. Robin still takes care of the outside work like mowing the lawn, weed whacking and plowing snow in the winter. I do the weeding and trimming which I consider artistic. I love having a beautiful property and I am fussy about keeping it looking pretty, including our woods. Robin thinks I'm crazy to do some of the things I do to accomplish this, but it's my choice. What can I say? There will be tasks that you want to share like grocery shopping and other errands. Make them fun!

If you don't have a partner, you are probably doing everything yourself and I applaud you for being superwoman already. As you start to slow down or maybe you just don't want to do some things yourself anymore, don't be afraid to ask for help. If you have children, it's time to reach out. Is it time to hire outside help for tasks like lawn care or snow removal?

You're not admitting defeat but instead are moving to a new phase in your life. Make the adjustments you require when you require them. Life is too short to suffer doing "maintenance" if you don't have to. Still cleaning your home? If you don't love it, hire someone to take over. Having someone come in every two weeks, will take the bulk of the burden off you and you will have the pleasure of employing someone who may make their living from cleaning. How about hiring a landscaper to come in and do a cleanup in the spring in your yard? It's a onetime yearly cost and then you can enjoy maintaining your gardens. Some of these services are priceless. There is help out there so reap the seeds you've sown over the years.

What tasks have you learned in retirement? You'll be surprised to see how much you will enjoy them now that you aren't pressured for time or limited by exhaustion!

Take the time to think about the tasks around your home and how you might change them going forward. Don't spend all your time working at home unless you love it!

1. What tasks would you like to take on or learn?

2. What tasks would you like to ask for help with?

3. What tasks would you like to consider hiring outside help for?

Notes:

Chapter Four

Reading List

I like keeping a list on my white board right in front of my eyes because I also enjoy reading multiple books at once. I also like to keep the titles of books that others recommend on my list so I can read them in the future. I have different categories: personal growth, factual and pleasure. Getting a library card and joining the book club at my local library gave me so much pleasure, intellectually, socially and emotionally. This is something I would recommend for everyone. I also continue reading books that I have in my personal library that I've collected over the years.

If you are not a reader, consider starting. I had a library card when I was younger but let that expire as my career took off. Instead of borrowing books, I would buy any books that I was interested in reading. Most of them were personal growth or business. I didn't feel like I had much time to squeeze pleasure reading into my schedule. Guess what? Now I had time! The business books are now gathering dust on my book shelves. I would like to give them away and have found a group called "Women in Technology". I talked to one of their members and she recommended I give them to her for their next networking event. She agreed to set up a table with the books on it so that other members can peruse and take the ones that are of interest to them. I was thrilled. Some I had never read and have no desire to read them now. I thought I might change my mind in the future but how important is it really? It's time to say good bye to them and give them to other women would might appreciate and learn from them just like I did.

Personal growth is another matter. I don't ever want to stop growing. The topics have changed a little bit but not drastically. I am a very spiritual person so any books on that are high on the list. I also want to stay current. Right now I start my day with an inspirational book and I just read one page each morning. I recently read "2121 Funny Stories and How to Tell Them" that was written in the 1940's! Obviously I own this book since it took me forever to get through and I was amazed by what they thought was funny in the 40's. I have found books at yard sales and other second hand "opportunities" very inexpensively and have added them to my collection. If you find one that you really want to start your day with, it's still okay to buy it or maybe a friend has a copy they could lend you. Don't forget to return it to them though. I have lost many books that way (I hope they are still circulating among friends.) I find starting my day with inspiration sets the tone for the rest of the day in a positive manner.

I also love ending my day with reading. This is where my pleasure reading really shines. It gives me a chance to clear my mind of any daily thoughts or worries and I sleep like a log. Of course, if the book has captured my attention, I may take time during the day to enjoy it in my favorite chair or on the porch during the nice weather. I know so many people who keep their phones with them always and scroll for hours before bedtime and then complain they can't sleep soundly. Big mistake! Reading for pleasure is so grounding, giving you opportunities to imagine and experience things beyond your wildest dreams. Take advantage of it.

I also like to read a page or two of a learning book each day. I start my day with one and end my day with a different one. The morning is for inspiration and grounding. The one right before I lay my head on the pillow is for learning. An example from me is "Art in Everyday Life". I read a couple pages before I go to bed and think about it. It doesn't attract worry, just thought-provoking insight.

I'd love to share a little more about the library with you. I have lived in my little town for almost 20 years and never visited the library until I retired. I had seen a sign for it on the road but never went in the little building. When I first left work, visiting it was at the top of my list. I was so pleasantly surprised by what I found. This tiny building contained so many books and movies at my disposal. That is what I expected. What I didn't expect was the kindness and friendship that developed with the librarians. They are so accommodating when I go in and eager to make recommendations on books, authors and everything the library has to offer. I joined the book club and met other amazing women (but men are welcome) to discuss our current books. This evolved into talking about how the themes in the books were relevant to our lives. We began sharing stories of our own experiences and friendships began. I can't wait until it starts again in the fall.

Did you know that your library also offers other benefits? Ours has special activities like a cookie decorating class, a painting class, a "Witches Brew" tea at Halloween time where we even made a special tea to take home, a reading contest with prizes and monthly crafts to take home and create on your own. These are just a few that I can remember participating in the last year. And here's another crazy thing…..they are all free! And I even won the reading contest twice. Don't underestimate the impact this establishment and practice can have for a happy retirement.

Think about how you might incorporate reading into your new found freedom. If you have never had a "reading practice", that's okay. Start small and see if you like it. Maybe get a simple daily devotional and read a page when you get up in the morning. Visit your local library and get a library card. Talk to the librarians about your interests and see what they might recommend. Borrow a movie or two. Instead of reading a handheld book, maybe you'd like to try an audio book. They have a whole collection there or you can even borrow them online through the library's app, Libby. If they don't have a book in house that you would like to read, they can order it in and notify you when they receive it. There are so many options to explore and they are all available through your local library for free. If you own your home, you have been paying taxes to support this entity, so why not take advantage of it?

If you are ready to pare down your own collection, offer them to the library, a senior center, a youth center, the YMCA, any facility that might benefit from them. It's best to check with them first though before you bring in boxes of books. They will let you know if they can take them and will appreciate your proactivity.

Enjoy transporting yourself to other worlds, times and experiences from the comfort of your home.

Think about how reading might become part of your daily activities.

1. Do you have a library card? If not, get one.

2. Think about what types of books you might be interested in. List them here.

3. Do you prefer reading a handheld book or are you interested in trying a tablet? If you would prefer a tablet, research the types available and purchase one if you are interested in trying it.

4. Consider breaking your reading out into different types during the day. Start with a book that inspires you like a devotional or daily quotes. If you are spiritual / religious, consider reading the Bible front to back or pull out scripture to match your mindset.

5. Ask your local librarian what your library offers and jump in where you feel ready.

6. Join or start a book club.

Notes:

Chapter Five

Exercise

Exercise is key for a well-rounded retirement. You don't have to run a marathon or work out like a maniac but there are many aspects of activity that are available. If you are 65+ and have a Medicare Advantage plan, you are most likely eligible for Silver Sneakers which gives you free access to the YMCA and other gyms. Check with your Medicare Consultant or your plan online. If you have a different medical insurance plan, check to see if Silver Sneakers is included. The YMCA offers physical, social and artistic growth. You can even learn about nutrition. I have increased my strength, met some wonderful people and have a safe place to work out. I also still go to a class through adult community education in my school system with a friend who is not yet retired. I can take advantage of the senior discount and enjoy those classes in the evening for a minimal amount. Don't forget about your non-retired friends! Staying fit is the key to good health and a good outlook on life.

When my husband stopped working nine years ago, it was his dream to "just sit". He worked in a factory for most of his career which meant he was on his feet for the majority of the time and walked a concrete floor, day in and day out. Now he sits in the corner of our kitchen most days, browsing his phone, looking at miscellaneous apps for news and entertainment, sometimes not even feeling motivated enough to get dressed. I know he is not the only one to relish the privilege to "do nothing" in retirement. I was still working and couldn't wrap my head around this practice. Does that mean it's wrong? Not for him but I thought that would not be my ideal hobby. Once I got to retire, something unexpected happened to him. His body betrayed him from so much sitting and I was disappointed.

I have always been devoted to exercise since I was young. I wasn't really a "gym person" but I loved classes. When I was younger, I would do classes that were on TV to stay fit. I remember my mom razzing me about it because like Robin, she did not value physical activity. As video tapes and DVD's became available, I would purchase the ones that featured exercises that I enjoyed. I loved Richard Simmons and his "Sweatin' to the Oldies" and I did them every day after work. My children became used to seeing me work out and I even took them to "Mommy and Me" classes when they were little. I moved to exercise through Adult Education at our local school once the kids were old enough to be more self-sufficient. I've done jazzercize, body sculpting, Zumba and yoga looking for classes that were inexpensive or even free. In the summers, our local YMCA offers "Fitness in the Park" and I enjoyed those classes all over our area. I even did online yoga in the middle of the day at home when I was working remotely to break up all that sitting. When we lived in the suburbs, I would get up at 5:30 a.m. and walk the streets before getting ready for work to clear my head and keep moving. You are probably seeing a theme here. My husband and I are opposites when it comes to physical activity. When I retired, that didn't change my desire to stay fit and active because I wanted to enjoy all those things I had been waiting to do once I was free from the 9 to 5.

One of my dreams had always been to join the YMCA. When we met with our Medicare consultant to talk about healthcare for the future, she educated us on the Silver Sneakers program. Not only can you have a free membership at the Y but it is also extended to many other gyms. I couldn't believe it! As I said earlier, I am not really a "gym person" but the Y really attracted my attention. In the month of my 65th birthday, I dragged Robin to the Y closest to our home for a tour. The facility was only four years old and it was amazing. It has two floors with multiple opportunities to stay fit depending on your desires. They have scheduled classes Monday through Friday and our tour director loaded the app on my phone so I could see them for each day. When you click on them you can even add them to your calendar as a recurring appointment. She showed us everything: all the equipment, the pool, the gym, the indoor walking track, the locker rooms and the areas where they have classes. The possibilities felt endless. We signed up and got started the next day. My favorite classes are the Silver Sneakers classic, Silver Sneakers yoga, Zumba, Boom Muscle, Ener-chi and a drumming class. I will probably try others that are earlier in the day but I'm not there yet. I still value my leisure time in the mornings. I love the walking track because it's flat and cushioned so good for the knees and safety.

Robin quickly faded so I was on my own. I began introducing myself to other participants and began making acquaintances. I really clicked with one of the women in a class and we began a true friendship. You are never too old to make new friends! She was also newly retired so we were experiencing it together. We took other classes at the Y as well. They offer craft classes and nutrition classes. Again, once you join you can get as involved as you want and emails will arrive with offerings to take advantage of. You will even qualify for a few personal trainings through Silver Sneakers to target the areas you are most interested in. Oh, did I mention that Robin and I also took ballroom dancing classes for free through the Y? We did but Robin could not continue because of his knees. I was grateful that he tried but again, his lifestyle did not support it. Those classes were also a lifelong desire for me so I was disappointed but it was not to be for right now. My goal is to go at least twice a week but on slow weeks where I'm not busy with other activities, I go four times. I hope you will consider this wonderful benefit to stay fit and healthy. It is priceless. And the social aspect is equally important. Now that your lifestyle has changed, it's important to spend time with others and this is the perfect place to make new friends with as little or as much interaction as you would like. I couldn't believe how much fun it is.

So that's my "new" exercise commitment but don't discount the old practices if they still serve you. As I said, I also enjoy the opportunities through Adult Education from my school district. My friend, Kathie and I have been doing classes there for years and since she is still working and not yet 65, we continue to sign up. The classes we take have changed throughout the years though. We started with an intense body sculpting class, then moved to Zumba and now we are enjoying water aerobics. Our bodies do change over time and it's critical to take good care of them, especially our joints. Some of you may be "beasts" and would like to continue or even start running marathons, cross fit or other intense programs. If so, go for it! But again, be aware of your body and take it slow with an expert if it's new to you. I have learned to respect my limitations but to also push myself to go further, slowly and intentionally.

Think about what might work for you. I still do yoga, especially on retreats and I love it but not "power yoga". I do it more for flexibility and strength but not anything too intense. Whatever you do (and I hope you do something), start slow and smart and build from there. If it hurts, modify but don't stop. Maybe walking is your thing. Enjoying nature, especially in nice weather, is not only physical but good for your soul. Find your bliss but keep moving. Love to garden in the summer? Great! My new friend, Linda took time off from the Y for the summer months to care for her gardens as well as a large vegetable garden at her parents' house. It's whatever motivates you to stay physically fit so you can enjoy everything in your life. You will not regret it.

List ideas on how you will stay active in your retirement. Remember, there are formal exercise programs as well as casual ones.

-

-

-

1. What are you already doing to stay fit? List the activities and how you feel about them. Love them? Tired of them?

2. What new activities would you like to add to your routine? List them along with where you would like to do them.

3. Investigate the gyms in your area and set up tours. Make notes on what you liked or disliked about each one. Remember to join Silver Sneakers if you are 65+ and ask them if they participate in the program so that you can join for free.

Notes:

Chapter Six

Give Back

It took me time to find the "right" opportunities for me. I was coming down from a 47-year intense career so jumping right into a strenuous volunteer practice felt overwhelming. Everyone is different though. I found opportunities at church and even going back to church regularly was a big change for me. I explored other options and I knew I would find the right ones in the future as I continued to explore. You should, too. It doesn't mean you have to "run something" but just adding your talents to an organization is very meaningful. Don't underestimate your impact, no matter how small.

So what are you passionate about? When I went to that retreat on "rest" when I first retired, there was a woman there who had retired the previous year. When she first shared about why she had come to the retreat, she confessed that she was totally burned out from volunteering! I sat there with my mouth hanging open and my eyes wide. As she continued with the details, even I felt overwhelmed by her commitments. I think that's why I chose to really think about where I wanted to spend my time. I made a list of agencies that I had always thought, "if only I had more time, I'd love to volunteer there".

My first priority was going back to church. I have always enjoyed practicing my faith since I was a child. My parents had me baptized as a baby and took me to Sunday School until we moved to another town when I was ten. There was a church across the street from our home, so I took myself there so that I may learn from them. Crazy right? From there I had many twists and turns with different churches that I attended depending on where we lived. I have settled into the Wesleyan church down the road from me. I attended services years ago but then my schedule got so busy and my responsibilities at home increased so I "let it go". I always thought that when I didn't have to do everything on weekends that I would return and I did. For me, church is a place to learn and deepen my faith. I am also very spiritual so I struggle with some of the beliefs of the Wesleyans but the people and the pastor are kind and loving. I always say I am not here to judge anyone; therefore, I take what I like and leave the rest.

When I renewed my commitment to church, I began to attend worship almost every week and began tithing, although I did not "join" formally. I was committed to understanding what the church was all about now before I put both feet in. I had already tried being a Sunday School teacher, but that is not my calling. What I did find comfortable was the "quick hit" opportunities, singing in the Easter choir, making bunny tails for the Easter baskets we were distributing and throwing my hat in the ring to become a greeter and lay reader. Volunteering at church is another wonderful way to meet new people and build relationships in a loving way.

Once the summer hit, I stopped going. They moved the service up and here I was on my porch enjoying the beautiful weather and my commitment waned. Did my faith fade? Absolutely not. I think my struggle with some of their beliefs prevented me from committing. I am very spiritual and I pray daily. I did return in the spring and have been going faithfully ever since. However you treat this part of your life is up to you. It truly is a personal choice but it must be somewhere you are comfortable. And again, if you aren't, you can leave and try another church or different form of worship. The choice is yours and it can be fluid.

If church is not your thing, maybe there are other spiritual places for you to consider like yoga studios, meditation groups, self-help groups and even retreats. If you try something and don't feel comfortable, that's okay. You can stop going and continue your journey to find what does work for you.

I decided to dip my toe into our local theater as a volunteer. I didn't explore it until a year after my formal retirement. I have always enjoyed attending events and live plays at this historic theater so why not? I filled out a form online and heard nothing. Okay..... When I was purchasing tickets for a musical at their box office, I told the attendant what I had done but that I hadn't heard anything and it had been months. She excitedly informed me that they were having a volunteer appreciation event that week and invited me to come. What an amazing coincidence! I asked if I should sign up but she said, no, just come, so I did. The event was lovely and I met another woman who was also there as a "first time volunteer". Great! We sat together, enjoyed some food and listened to the Executive Director talk about the venue, their goals for the coming year and how volunteers impact their success. I was so excited. But here's the rub. It wasn't really designed as a new volunteer orientation so I asked lots of questions and got what I needed to get started as a volunteer. It was clumsy and uninformative but I decided to forge ahead and I signed up to work at their next event. This could turn into a long story but the bottom-line is don't expect volunteer opportunities to be as organized as your work places may (or may not) have been. I was able to join in because I was passionate, confident and not afraid to ask questions. Don't let their lack of organization discourage you or make you think they don't care. They probably do but are overwhelmed so do what you can to help and see if you like it. And guess what....if you don't, you don't have to continue. You're a volunteer! But do get over the bumps first and give it a chance for you to get comfortable before making your final decision.

I checked out another center in our community by going to their annual meeting but I could feel how tight knit their team of volunteers was. They gave no clear path on how to become a volunteer despite each reporting group confessing that they are looking for more help. It didn't feel right at that moment but I am keeping them in mind for the future. One way to explore your options is to become a member of the organizations you are interested in. That gives you that opportunity to attend events to see if it is a fit for you and support them financially at the same time.

Community organizations are always looking for help. The Salvation Army has always been at the top of our contribution list. How about your historical society, the Lion's Club or library? Ask your friends where they enjoy volunteering. The message is to explore before jumping in with both feet. If you feel ready to throw your hand up, do it and see where it takes you. If you start performing duties that you don't like, guess what? You can be honest with the agency and stop. Maybe there are other jobs within that agency or maybe it's not your thing. Either way, your time is valuable so if you are not getting pleasure out of volunteering, don't waste it. But should you contribute somewhere, you will be appreciated and receive so many blessings from your heartfelt work. I can almost guarantee it!

1. Make a list of the organizations that interest you.

   -
   -
   -
   -
   -
   -
   -
   -
   -

2. Which one would you like to try first? Write it down and begin researching what type of volunteer opportunities there are in that organization. Put them here along with who to contact to find out more. Begin the process and see where it takes you. If you don't like it, it's okay to drop out and move on.

   -
   -
   -
   -
   -
   -
   -

Notes:

Chapter Seven

Learn New Things (Hobbies)

During my first year of retirement, I have explored painting with watercolors, cookie decorating, making crafts, drawing, cooking and baking. I am also working on my gardening skills and writing. Am I done? Not even close. I love exploring new things. You never know where your talents lie until you give something a try. Many successful artists, authors, inventors, etc. didn't even start until later in life. You can, too!

You may wonder how you might learn new skills. I know I did. Well, you are retired at an amazing time because you can learn anything on the internet via You Tube, TikTok or just by doing a general Google search. I'd like to share some of my experiences.

Art has always been one of my passions. When I was in school, I excelled in the art classes I took but the further I got into my studies, it got pushed aside for academics. "How can you make a living with art?" my parents would say. "You've got to be practical." Their idea of practical was secretarial courses so that I could get a job out of high school, find a husband to take care of me and become a full-time wife and mother. That didn't work out quite well for me but that's another story, as Robin would say. I did as my parents instructed so as my life became busier and busier with family and career, I put my sketch books aside and focused on other things.

Once I retired, I thought it would be the perfect time to begin again. I brought out all the art supplies that I had accumulated, mostly for my grandchildren to enjoy and thought about which medium I would like to dive into first. In my past, I had concentrated on drawing but I thought it might be fun to learn how to paint. I had done some of those "paint nights" that had become so popular from time to time so I learned a little bit through those but that was not enough for me. When I shipped my laptop and other equipment back to my company after July 1, HR sent me labels and a recommendation of the closest shipper to my house. I followed those directions and discovered that we had an art gallery only ten miles or so from my home. I couldn't believe it when I walked in. They pay their rent by being a UPS and FedEx shipper but their passion is supporting local artists by preparing and displaying their work. They let me know that they were doing "artist circles" on Wednesdays throughout the summer and invited me to join. They were planning on having a different artist each week to teach and showcase their specialties to the participants. How wonderful! I came each week and even invited my niece to join me along the way and while it didn't turn out exactly as they wished, it was a wonderful opportunity for me to learn from established artists since Sarah (my niece) and I were the only ones who ever came. Disappointing for them, lucky for us. Our focus was watercolors and I received recommendations from the artists on where they buy their supplies and the techniques they use. It was a hidden gem.

I continued practicing at home after the sessions were over. The key to having an enjoyable practice, I soon discovered, was having a comfortable space for me to work where I didn't have to put everything away after each session. I took over our family room. I keep the doors closed when I'm not in there to keep the dogs out. This has enabled me to work comfortably, even for an hour without having the hassle of the set up and clean up each time. I even have a TV in there so I can put on music or listen to a show in the background. I guess I could even put on a You Tube tutorial so I could learn and follow along right there in my makeshift studio. As I practiced, I affirmed to myself that I was practicing and that perfection may not be achievable. The beautiful thing about art is that it is self-expression. The beauty comes from within so whatever you create is an extension of you.

If you are interested in art, check out your local galleries to see if they have classes, adult education, your community college or even your YMCA, library and senior centers. Opportunities are everywhere for this particular hobby. There are also many different mediums. Maybe charcoals or pastels for drawing are your thing. Watercolors, oils and acrylics could be fun to try for painting but let me warn you, oils take forever to dry and will not come out of whatever they are on easily. There are opportunities for sculpture, wood burning, woodworking, carving, almost anything you can think of. You can even paint rocks. It's whatever gives you pleasure and serenity. You will find your bliss with continued exploration.

Cooking and baking have become a lovely part of my life, not just a necessity to stay alive. I have deepened my skills with cooking by trying new recipes that intrigue me from the internet. (Be careful when following links.) I find now that if I have an ingredient that I want to use in a dish, I can look up a recipe that includes it. I love fresh vegetables and the summer is perfect for either growing them yourself or heading to the nearest farmer's market to purchase what is ready and make something delicious with it. Now that I have the time, I can plan on making more complicated dishes during the week when my schedule is light. And don't forget to save those leftovers. Chinese food containers are perfect for creating serving size leftovers for quick meals. Stack them up in your refrigerator or freezer and enjoy them as needed.

I also love baking but since weight control is top of mind, I'm careful about what I make. Instead of stacking up the treats at home for me and Robin, I make things when we have company or are invited somewhere so everyone can enjoy some and there isn't so much left over. I love "The

Great British Baking Show" and creating some of those dishes has been fun, especially because they are not as heavy on sugars as we are stateside. Everyone enjoys the special treats since baking seems to be a lost skill with the younger generation. I hope it makes a comeback. I have also taken classes on cookie decorating, "no cook" cooking and other nutritional offerings through the library and the YMCA. Keep your eyes open. It's also healthier to make goodies from scratch since the preservatives will not be included.

Think about gardening. You may not have a green thumb but it can be very rewarding. As I have already mentioned, having my gardens professionally landscaped to give me a fresh start was invaluable to me. Since I no longer have the strength or desire to do the heavy lifting, I also invite that landscaper to come back each year to do a spring clean-up. After that I'm on my own, taking care of the trimming and weeding. I consider my gardens a work of art and I feel great pride in them. But I no longer spend hours and hours at a time in the hot sun working on them on weekends. Instead, I divide my time into multiple days so that I can truly enjoy it and not overdo it. That is so important at this stage of our lives. I have also enjoyed adding additional plants each year, some perennials and some annuals. I am loving this evolving creation.

Is gardening in your yard too much for you? Or maybe you live in a space without a yard. That's okay. How about creating lovely pots each year to adorn your entrance, balcony or porch? There is still so much pleasure in bringing nature closer to you. I admit I do not have a vegetable or fruit garden. I do have a few fruit trees but that is it. Since we do live in a rural area, fresh produce is plentiful and growing it myself is not one of my callings. Is it yours? If so, it can be as big or as small as you would like it to be. How about just patio tomatoes or an herb garden? Once the harvest comes in, canning and freezing your goodies can also be enjoyable and fun, especially with a friend. The possibilities are endless and you will have healthy and delicious options all year long.

The last "new thing" I wanted to share with you is exploring the wonderful world of writing. When I retired, I wanted to write a book. I thought about it before I actually stopped working and the topic I kept coming back to was what to expect when you retire (this book). I had never really read anything about what my retirement might look like and all I had ever heard from others was that they wanted to travel. Of course! Everyone wants to travel and you should not wait until you retire to do so but I do understand that desire to travel whenever you want to and for how long you might want to be gone. When we are working, we are usually restricted by vacation time.

Now that we are in the age of remote work, people are not as restricted as we once were and can explore different areas and work remotely. I always felt conflicted by that since when I was on vacation, I wanted to be free from my job to truly immerse myself in the area I was vacationing in. My daughter, Jessie is a remote worker and she travels to other areas as an international pet-sitter. She found an agency online that gives you the opportunity to pet sit and live in that client's house for free. She doesn't get paid for doing it but having a place to stay rent-free was enticing for her. She has done it in Colorado and even England. This could be a great opportunity for you as a retiree to explore other areas inexpensively. If you are still working and work remote, you could give it a try, too. The website for more information is https://www.trustedhousesitters.com/.

So, back to writing. As my career was winding down, I began journaling, documenting everything I was doing on a daily basis and the lessons I was learning along the way. I was thinking that could be my book. Wouldn't everyone be interested in how my retirement unfolded? I decided to journal for exactly one year. Once the daily log was complete, I would then write an epilogue and call it a book. I decided to let my youngest daughter review it when I was done. As I read one of my entry's she began to glaze over. Was it a mistake to share it with a 38-year-old? Maybe, but she gave me some really good insight on what she believed others (and herself) would really like to hear more about. Hmmm....I thought about her feedback and evaluated what that might look like. She gave me very specific direction on what I should eliminate (the daily log) and what I might expand upon. I was hurt at first, but the more I thought about it, I knew she was right. So I took my original book which was 331 pages long and did a complete rewrite. And that is what you have in your hands right now. I hope she was right.

So why do I share this story with you about the journey of my book? It's because it is just that….a journey. Did I really think I could sit down and write a bestseller for my first attempt? Yeah, I kind of did. But the journey has been wonderful. Do you have an idea for a book? How about an article for your local newspaper? Maybe you would like to share something via a BLOG. I also love poetry and I wrote a special poem in a book that I passed along to my great granddaughter that her father had treasured when he was a little boy. That might be something that would tickle your fancy. Maybe it's a story of your travels and some of the amazing places that you've been. How about a mystery, a novel or a self-help book on a topic you are passionate about? Whatever comes into your mind or heart is what you should focus on. Authors do get ideas and when they can't get them out of their heads or when they are so detailed, and they can't believe they thought of them, then that's your book. Get writing before you forget everything and it gets passed onto someone else.

So those are just some of the new things I have learned in my first year of retirement. They certainly won't be the last. Whether your heart longs for a hundred new talents or just one, this is the time to take the plunge and give it a go. If you're not an expert right out of the gate, so what? This is for your pleasure. And if you try something and you hate it, let it go. It may not be for you. The beauty of retirement is time so as you learn, take the time to walk away from a project when you get frustrated or tired and go back when you are refreshed. You will have a completely different perspective and your renewed energy may be just what the doctor ordered to finish what you started. Think like a child. Ask questions and research what you want to try. That's half the fun! Now get out there and try something new.

I hope I've inspired you to try new things. Now list the things that come to mind. Next to each one, write down how you might get started. Are supplies required? How about some sort of tutorial? Can you take a class or find something online? Keep it simple at first, especially if you are trying something new. See if you like it before you invest too much money into it.

Notes:

Summary

Now you've heard about the basic categories that I came up with before I retired. I hope some of my activities have inspired you to start dreaming and planning your own retirement and that you will think of other categories that you would like to focus on. You may not be "making money" like you used to, but don't let that be your #1 focus. Your spending will change with your new lifestyle. I am in pretty good shape financially, not rich by any means but not scraping by either. I spend my money on things that mean the most to me. I don't waste it on luxuries to impress others and I don't use it to support my family. That's not my job. They are living their best lives, just the way they envision them (not the way I envision them). Enjoy the fruits of your labor and make these next days more fulfilling than you ever imagined. You've earned it and you deserve it!

Are there other categories that you would like to focus on? If so, list them below with the actions you would like to take to get started. This is your time to shine!

Part 2

Invaluable lessons I would like to share

Chapter Eight

No One is Perfect And Neither Are You

This statement is true for everyone. It's not a negative statement on what a terrible person you are. Instead, it is affirmation that we are all doing our best every day.

When I was younger, my parents were very critical of me. I know they did it out of love but it still hurt. My dad was very intelligent and wanted us to be as well so that we might have countless opportunities in our future. I studied hard for each subject and I was better in some than others but I almost always got straight A's on my report cards. (I did get a C in Health as a senior but that was because I skipped that class weekly and when I confronted my teacher about my grade, she declared that if I put in any effort, I could have gotten an A. I did do all of my homework and got straight A's on it as well as the tests but she was looking for effort. Oh well, I can't go back but it did ruin my perfect record.) My dad was disappointed anytime I didn't get a perfect grade and it put so much pressure on me as a child. Now as an adult I still try to be perfect. I'm finally loosening up in retirement.

Perfection is not achievable so just stop trying. You will encounter many people in your life, hopefully daily, that will do things differently than you might. So what? That's what makes us all so unique and interesting. You don't have the best plan or solution for others. You may want to share your wisdom with younger people, especially those in your family but do it with kindness. Here are some examples I have used:

- That sounds interesting. Tell me more.
- I think I understand. Can I ask a few questions for clarification?
- I hear what you're saying. That happened to me once. Would you like to hear how I handled it?
- I can see how passionate you are about that. I hope it all works out for you. Let me know if there is anything I can do to help. (Be careful on this last part though. Don't just take over, especially financially.)
- I see you are struggling with this situation. Would you like to hear about when I experienced the same thing or would you just like me to listen?

These are just a few approaches when someone comes to you with an issue or may just be talking about one. Sometimes people just want us to listen, not solve. If someone asks what they should do, it's safer to share what you might do or have done and not just tell them what to do. That way you won't own the results if it doesn't work out. You can ask them what they have already tried and what the results were or who they may have talked to for advice. Remember, we are still learning every day as well.

My children and grandchildren have not lived their lives as I may have done but they are learning and flourishing in their own way. They have seen me struggle and they have seen me thrive and I know that they have incorporated my knowledge and experiences into their journeys. That makes me grateful and proud. When my adult children come to me for advice, I use many of the statements above to start the conversation. Be careful when criticizing their partners, friends and especially their children. Love and support them in any way that you can.

When it comes to friends, acquaintances, neighbors, etc., this is where you want to be very careful. Again, some will just want an ear to vent. Be careful with your words so as not to hurt them or be too critical. Even when people are mad about someone's behavior, that doesn't mean they are out of their life. When you hear complaints, it's best to say something like, I'm so sorry that your feelings have been hurt, that you are struggling or that you are not happy. It's best to revert back to questions instead of advice. You might say something like "how would you like this situation to change?" or "what steps would you like to take next?". Affirming how they feel is imperative. Discounting their emotions or brushing them away is not the way to go even if the circumstance seems trivial. Remember, we are not trained therapists. We are friends who care so showing compassion rather than judgment is what someone who loves them would do.

Love everyone despite their flaws and support them, whatever that may look like. With every one you encounter, always be kind, even with grouchy people. You don't know how they got there. Your kindness will go a long way.

Think about how you might do one kind thing a day for someone else. Start with you! Record them here and acknowledge how your relationship may have changed because of it. You truly do make a difference in other peoples' lives as well as your own.

Notes:

Chapter Nine

Self-Care

Self-care should still be a priority. If you're not happy, no one else around you will be either. Take a day off when you want to. Keep getting massages if you like them. Take good care of your feet by getting pedicures regularly. You still deserve all these pleasures if they make you happy.

When I first retired, I considered dropping some of my self-care routines. Do I really need a massage every two or three weeks? This had been my practice for many years while I was working. Sitting at a desk or in an airplane wreaked havoc on my body and I began getting massages to relieve stress and muscle aches. But in retirement shouldn't all my stress and aches be gone? I wish I could say they were. So, I kept going to my massage therapist and thought when I get to the point of feeling Zen, I can stop. Well, guess what? A couple of things happened.

First, it has been over a year since I stopped working and my shoulders are still a mess with bumps and "railroad tracks" as Patti calls them. She explained that it took many years to "get them" and they will not go away overnight. Boo! The second interesting thing that happened was that my Medicare Advantage insurance supports massages, too. I get $250 per year towards them. Well, if my insurance supports massages then it sounds like more of a necessity than a luxury, doesn't it? Check your insurance to see if you have an allowance as well.

The second thing I continue to treat myself to is pedicures. I don't really like manicures as much since I like to keep my fingernails short and unpolished but my feet are a different story. Not only do I enjoy the cleaning and massaging (seeing a theme here?) but cutting my toenails has become difficult. I am prone towards ingrown toenails on my big toes and foot health is critical to a happy life. I don't get polish during the winter months but when sandals come out, I enjoy having pretty toes. As we get older, they need all the help they can get. I go every six weeks and that keeps my feet in good shape.

Speaking of feet, wearing the right shoes has become critical. When did my feet start hurting with certain shoes? I can't put my finger on it but I now have to be careful with what I put on my feet. Flip flops for the most part are not good, especially the cheap ones. High heels are out…. period. I wear sneakers on most days and I finally found a brand that was perfect for me called Hoka. I went to a store that specializes in foot care. When you go in, they not only measure your feet but they also measure how your foot hits the ground and your gait. Then they bring out shoes they believe will feel and fit the best. There is no rush and it is almost as good as going to a specialist. I guess they are. The sneakers are not cheap but they are worth every penny. Mine have thick soles, arches and a large toe box. These three things are critical for my feet. Since I wear them to the YMCA to work out and almost anytime I know I'll be walking more than sitting, having a good pair of sneakers is necessary for comfort and motivation to keep going. I also don't like sandals that are plastic on the insoles. My feet tend to rub on them when I walk and they become very uncomfortable very quickly. I do have a comfortable pair of fashion boots for cooler weather and of course, winter boots since I live in a changeable climate. The bottom line is comfort over fashion. If you have shoes that are uncomfortable and you can't wait to take them off, donate them or throw them out. It's just not worth it anymore.

Let's talk about your hair. Do you get it professionally done or do you do it at home? I am lucky because my youngest daughter is a hair stylist. She has been doing my hair for 23 years and it has been a roller coaster, especially in the beginning. When she was still in school learning her craft, we had many scary hair flops! I've had crazy colors and cuts that were not optimal, but over the years she has become a master. Have you kept your hair natural? If so and you love it, great! If you are coloring your hair and you love it, keep that process going. My natural color is white now and I am not ready for that drastic change since I have been coloring my hair a dark brown since it started going grey in my 20's. I even have fun colors added like purple, pink and blue. De, my daughter and stylist likes to keep my hair current and so do I. Have fun with yours. Right now my hair is long and between the color and the style, it gives me a youthful appearance. Is that why I do it? Yes! I want to look in the mirror each morning and feel good about myself. That is the goal with many self-care practices.

De also waxes my eyebrows and upper lip to keep them looking feminine. Now even my eyebrows have become lighter, so she also dyes them to match my hair. Just the dark brown, not the fun colors – LOL. Self-care is all about feeling good, about your appearance and physically. Don't give that up unless you absolutely must because of the expense or if you are ready for a change.

I think those are the most important self-care regimens that I practice regularly. I also enjoy other fun activities occasionally like salt cave sessions, gong sound baths, wellness retreats and foot massages but those are sporadic. I don't worry about how much they cost anymore because I can afford them and I prioritize them over other things. Retirement is all about priorities! If you do have a tight budget, add a line for self-care. It doesn't have to be extravagant, but knowing you will do something for yourself, will boost your self-confidence and your joy.

If you want to do something, do it as soon as possible. I remember reading about saving certain "things" for special occasions only and the point of the snippet was to encourage people to use them today and not wait. Wow! That hit me hard years ago and I began the practice of enjoying those special things regularly. We use our good dishes whenever we have company, including kids. The wine glasses are a regular with the kids, too. The tablecloth my grandma gave me? It's on our table now and we use that table for all our meals. I do wash it weekly but I enjoy it every time I sit down to eat. The vase that sat on my grandma's shelf and then my mother's until I "inherited" it? It never saw fresh flowers until I took it off my shelf and now it sits in the center of my dining room table fully adorned. Why not? I use all my things regularly so that I might enjoy them. I don't know if my children will want any of them and they'll probably just end up in an estate sale when my time comes. Checking the value of something (if you are convinced it's a valuable antique) is easy. The internet can tell you in a few minutes if it's something you should store or sell or just enjoy.

What else can you think of that might be something you treat yourself to in order to feel and look good? Don't stop! Modify if and when you are ready but don't deprive yourself just because you're not working anymore. You are still worthy!

1. What are the activities / services that you are currently participating in that you consider self-care? List them and beside each, write a short summary of why you love it or why you might want to give it up. Add the cost so you can evaluate each properly.

2. Is there any other self-care activities that you would like to try? List them and begin researching providers in your area. Add the pros and cons of each along with the cost. Make an appointment when you are ready.

3. Are there any special one-time activities that you would like to plan around self-care? How about a wellness retreat? A girls' weekend? List them and begin researching what might be available along with the details to make them happen. Don't forget to include whether you'd like to do them solo or who you might want to invite to come along with you.

Notes:

Chapter Ten

Take Care of Your Body

I have to admit I wasn't ready for all the attention I was going to get once I turned 65 and went on Medicare and a Medicare Advantage plan. I have always taken good care of my body by going for preventative appointments with a variety of medical professionals but when you turn 65, your care is amped up.

Let's start with your primary doctor. If you don't have one, get one today. Not only do they keep an eye on your body when you go to your appointment, they are the ones who coordinate your care. What does that mean? They check your vitals when you go in but they also chart them over time. They keep an eye on vaccinations that you will require like shingles, pneumonia, tinnitus and others that come along. These are critical to prevent serious illnesses, not to treat them. Just do it!

When I go to my doctor, they also require blood work to monitor my cholesterol and glucose. So far, so good. In fact, I just had my bloodwork done and my "bad" numbers went down. I am winning! I was on the cusp but not on any medications to date. I work hard at that. My primary also keeps me on track with my bone density scans and the dreaded colonoscopy. They are equally important to staying healthy. The second is not fun but I go every three years since I am prone to polyps. Again, I hate it but I do it so that I will not get colon cancer.

As I mentioned, I am not on any prescription medication (which is rare) and I'd like to keep it that way for as long as possible. I do, however, take supplements: a multi-vitamin, vitamin D, calcium, fish oil, glucosamine chondroitin and magnesium daily. The doctor recommended all but the multi-vitamin, glucosamine chondroitin and magnesium but I have added them for my own comfort. I have taken a multi-vitamin for my whole life and have been pretty darn healthy. Why stop now? I recently added the glucosamine chondroitin for my joints and will inform my doctor next time I see him. The magnesium I added before bed. It is part of my night time routine and relaxes me for a peaceful sleep. It also keeps me regular in the pooping department so if you have issues with that, you may want to give it a try.

My health insurance also encourages me to have a home wellness visit each year. What???? I couldn't believe it! When did doctors start doing house calls again? I thought that went out in the 1950's. Well, my medical professional wasn't a doctor; he was a physician's assistant which is only a hair away from a doctor and as you know, many times when you go to your doctor, you only see a P.A., right? He checked everything including my height. This is interesting because at some time when I went to my doctor, the nurse recorded my height at 5'7". Really? I thought I was 5'8 ¾"? I let her know that but she argued with me and said I must have shrunk over the years. Okay…. Guess what? The P.A. that came to visit me also recorded my height at 5'8 ¾"! I asked him to verify it and he did. I let my new doctor know when I went for my introductory visit. This health insurance company is serious about keeping me healthy and I love it. When he left he said I was in excellent health for my age. He could have left out that last part, couldn't he? I even get gift cards for doing these preventative appointments. Check out what your insurance company offers.

I just mentioned that I have a new primary doctor. This is important, too. I received a call this year letting me know that my primary doctor was moving to a concierge medical practice to provide more personal care. It sounds nice but guess what? You have to pay out of pocket yearly for that personal care, to the tune of $2700! It is not covered by insurance and your co-pays and other fees stay the same. This service was new to me and if I had the extra money and health concerns, I might have considered it but at this time it seemed unnecessary. I went on my insurance website to research other primary doctors in my area and found one only a few miles from my house. I called for an appointment, had my introductory visit and loved him right away. He loves to be personally involved with his patients' care and believes that his oath is to serve our community. I filled out the paperwork to have my records transferred over, informed my old doctor that I was leaving and why, and let my insurance company know as well. All these steps are important. Remember, if you have a care provider that you are not comfortable with, it is your prerogative and your duty to find someone that cares about you and will take good care of you. You are not beholden to them.

Let's talk about the gynecologist next. I have always gone once a year which included a pap smear. A couple of years ago, my doctor stopped doing the pap smear yearly and I think he changed it to every other year because of my age and status. I have not had any problems so that seemed reasonable. At my last appointment (after I turned 65), he gave me the good news that I only need to see him every other year as well. I think that's the nicest thing he ever said to me! I guess there are a few good things that come with aging. He did, however, let me know that I should still get a mammogram yearly. Okay, that sounds fair. When I checked out, the receptionist told me that she would call me next year to make my appointment for the following year and provide me with a prescription for my mammogram. Okay. That works for me. Bottom line, even though you may not even be having sex anymore, going to your gynecologist is still critical for your "female" health. Don't let this go. It only takes a few minutes every other year.

How are your eyes doing? I have been wearing glasses since I was four years old. I did switch to contact lenses when I was a teenager until I required bifocals. I tried them as contact lenses but I didn't feel confident wearing them when I was traveling for work and attempting to read street signs before GPS's were invented. I still wear bifocals. I also had an issue with my pressure 20 years ago so I have been going to a specialist since that concern presented itself. Before that I had my eyes checked "when I couldn't see well anymore". Sometimes it was yearly and sometimes it was as long as five years. Eyes are another critical part of your body so treat them well! I now go to my specialist yearly since the pressure in my eyes has not changed. I have the beginning of a cataract in my left eye but it's not bad enough to fix it yet. My health insurance pays for my yearly exams and I get an allowance for my glasses. This is another area to stay up to date, especially if you drive. Buy glasses that you love! Don't cheap out. They are part of your body and one of the first things people see when they see you. Get glasses that fit well and give you confidence to face the world.

Lastly, let's talk about your teeth if you are lucky enough to still have some. When I was a child, the practice in my family was only to go a dentist if you had a problem. I went once when I chipped my tooth. When I was 20, I had an impacted wisdom tooth, so I went to the dentist to have it pulled. I was in the chair for hours as the dentist dug the tooth out. He gave me pain medication and boy, did I need it. Wow! I had never felt pain like that. It was one week before I got married and I was grateful that the pain finally dissipated by then. When I saw that dentist, he also informed me that I had periodontal disease. My teeth were perfect but my gums and the bones holding them in were not.

I went to the dentist for my first cleaning after that which took two visits since I had never been. He also recommended I go to a periodontist for treatment. Long story short, they scraped my teeth under my gums and did surgery to remove the bad stuff. After that I went to the dentist and the periodontist alternately every three months for the next 44 years. During that time, I had more teeth pulled because of my disease and I now have 19 left. Because of my losses, I began wearing partials to give me proper chewing capabilities. I have discontinued going to the periodontist after having a conversation with my dentist about a plan to keep the teeth I have left. He agreed to bring me in every four months for an intense cleaning. He was optimistic about his ability to keep my remaining teeth for as long as possible.

You may wonder why I stopped going to the periodontist since he is the expert on my disease. I found over the years that he cared more about pulling my teeth and replacing them with implants, than striving to keep the ones I have. I didn't like his plan. I continued to tell him that I wanted to keep my teeth but he just didn't listen. That's when I made the decision to stop going to him for my oral care and stick with my dentist exclusively. It may not be a perfect plan but it is the one that I am comfortable with. That is the bottom line when it comes to any kind of medical care. You know your body best. What I would encourage you to do is the same. Keep as many of your teeth for as long as you can. Dentures and implants are great but they are not as good as the teeth that are attached to your mouth. I may get to the point of dentures someday and if I do, I will ensure they fit me well and look as natural as possible. You should, too! Your teeth are important for good nutrition and enjoyment. Don't let them rot and fall out because you are afraid of the dentist. Put your big girl pants on and take care of your teeth and your smile. The bottom line is that you should also be active in your decisions about your oral care. If you are not confident in the providers you are going to, don't be afraid to express your concerns and get a second opinion or change providers if that makes you more comfortable.

In order to keep your body and your overall health in tip top shape, regular exercise is critical. So much so that most Medicare Advantage plans pay for gym memberships. It may be a program called Silver Sneakers (there is a website you can go on when you turn 65 to register and check your eligibility) or another type of benefit, and you can use it at the YMCA and other countless gyms. Check with your Medicare consultant for details. Start touring the facilities in your area and ask them if they take the program you have. Your insurance is devoted to keeping you healthy by giving this priceless gift to you. Take advantage of it. Find a place that you feel is convenient and comfortable.

I chose the YMCA to start. I love the beautiful facility and the offerings are wonderful. It is about 25 minutes from my house but I have found it worth it in so many ways. They offer classes each day that are geared towards "Silver Sneakers" participants as well as many other classes for everyone. They also have social events like dance classes, bingo, painting and craft classes and lunches and dinners. They have a walking track that is level and easy on the knees. They have a pool for swimming laps as well as aquatic classes. I strive to go at least three times a week and no, I don't stay for hours. I take a couple of classes and go home. In the winter, I like to use some of the machines like bikes and ellipticals. They have everything you could want and the staff are really sweet. Silver Sneakers even offers personal training sessions to get you started, included in the program. Mix your workouts up with cardio and strength training. We need both. As I said, regular gyms are also included so find the one(s) that you are excited to go to. You can join more than one.

And don't forget about adult community education at your local schools. The classes are inexpensive, with a senior discount if you are over 55. These are great if you have friends who may not be retired yet or members of the YMCA.

Don't forget to stay active in other ways as well. Love gardening? How about hiking with your grandchildren? Or just taking a walk or bike ride with friends. Don't be the elder always looking for a seat or declining events where walking is involved. Remember those comfortable sneakers? Wear those and join in the fun!

Being proactive with your health and your body will ensure you have a long and happy retirement. Your family will be grateful and so will you. You have the tools, so use them!

1. What doctors are you currently seeing regularly? List them here along with how often you go.

2. Are there parts of your care that you have let drop? Use my experience as a guideline. List those services below and take the time to research new providers on your insurance website or reach out to your Medicare consultant for candidates. List the ones you have researched and feel ready to contact below and make appointments. Don't forget to have all results sent to your primary doctor so they have a clear picture and see that you are up to date on necessary tests.

3. What are you currently doing for exercise? List the facilities you are currently using if you have any. If you are 65, are you a Silver Sneakers member yet? If not, go on their website and register. Begin researching facilities in your area that accept your medical insurance benefit or that are of interest if you are under 65. Write the pertinent information next to each and get started or continue your fitness journey.

Notes:

Chapter Eleven

If Something Is Broken, Fix It

This topic is pertinent with your body, your home, your car, your relationships, everything. Don't let things go, especially if you have the money to fix them. If you had a house cleaner when you retired, keep them on. Living in a clean home is a necessity, not a luxury.

Let's start with your body. At this point in our lives, we probably don't have the perfect body anymore. I know I don't and that's okay! But if something goes wrong with your body that is "fixable", do it. You already know that I wear glasses and I keep them current by going to the eye doctor to have my sight checked annually. When my prescription changes, I get a new pair of glasses. Don't settle for good enough with old glasses where you can no longer see well. If you have cataracts that are preventing you from vision good enough to pass an eye exam at the DMV, get them removed. Don't just stop driving. Clear eyesight is critical to your safety in so many ways. Keep it as sharp as possible.

One thing I had fixed this year was my little finger on my right hand. I have Dupuytren's contracture and my finger had permanently curled. This silly little thing affected me in a number of ways. When I shook someone's hand, I had to make sure I scooped their hand so that my finger wouldn't tickle their palm which is kind of creepy. When I splashed water on my face, I had to be careful not to poke myself in the eye. And don't even get me started on cutting the nail with clippers. It was awkward. I went to an orthopedic surgeon that participated in my insurance plan and received injections in my finger and palm to soften the fascia so the doctor could break the fascia and straighten my finger. Sounds painful? Yes, but it was worth it! Now my finger is straight and I can type more easily and no more awkwardness in any other way. It took months to get my flexibility back and to relieve the pain but with patience, lots of ice and focus on bending it, it's almost as good as new. I tell this story because this is something that was "elective" but it was important to me to have the ability to use this finger properly going forward.

What kinds of things have you let go? Have you lost your hearing? Have you gotten hearing aids or an implant to bring your hearing back so you can enjoy conversations, music, TV, etc. again? Do it! As we age, physical ailments may present themselves. Some will be emergencies where we don't have a choice except to fix it and some will be inconveniences that we could probably live with, but why? It could prevent you from living your best life, right?

If you are carrying extra weight like I am, now is the time to strip some of it away. I have enjoyed so many wonderful meals in my lifetime and when I was drinking, some amazing wines and liquors. I made the decision to cut alcohol from my life for many reasons. The calories were a small part of that. Now I am ready to lose weight to ease the stress on my knees and feet and to keep other maladies like type two diabetes and high cholesterol away. At 66, it's so much harder to lose weight than it was in my 30's, 40's and even 50's. I am not using any fad diet but instead, am making better choices. I have fallen in love with "baked oatmeal" for breakfast and I fill it with twice as much fruit as the recipe called for. I also make homemade vegetable soup which I have been having for lunch and I switch up the veggies I put in it each time I make it. Dinner is different every night but my goal is to have it vegetable heavy with protein and light carbs. I have restricted how much red meat I eat and focused more on chicken, venison and fish. I focus on ensuring I get enough healthy protein each day, around 120 grams. And here is the most difficult thing I have done. I have cut out my sugary snack in the evening. I love a cup of herbal tea before bed and instead of cookies or cake to go with it, I have nothing or if I am really hungry for something sweet, I will have a Hershey's miniature dark chocolate bar (42 calories). I stop eating early in the evening and I don't eat breakfast for at least 12 hours of fasting. During the day, if I get too hungry, I might have a 100-calorie bag of kettle corn or a 100-calorie frozen yogurt bar. I strive to eat whole foods and limit my processed foods. I drink tons of water, tea and celery juice. I am losing weight slowly but I am staying the course. If I hit a plateau, I change something in my diet. I knew it would be difficult but I celebrate each pound that I lose. When I am at a party or special occasion, I treat myself to a little something extra but I go right back to my plan afterwards. I think that's the goal. When I really want something, I eat it and enjoy it. No more beating myself up but understanding that what I put into my body can either increase my health or negatively affect it. The key is a happy balance.

If you would like to lose weight, be smart about it. Talk to your doctor. Talk to your friends who are slim and ask them how they keep their weight down. Focus on nutrition and eliminate as much sugar, processed foods and fried foods that you can. You'll find your taste buds will treasure the healthy foods that much more. Eat slowly and enjoy every bite. You can do it but be patient. Remember, every pound you lose will make a difference in your health. I started with a goal of 11 pounds and I continue to add new goals as I achieve each one. I haven't gotten to a weight I am comfortable with yet but I am getting closer. I knew it would be a battle but it is one that I would like to win. You can, too.

The next topic is kind of tricky for a few reasons: your home. Since you probably don't have a house full of people anymore, your utilization of your home changes. I live in a 2000 square foot home with four bedrooms and three bathrooms. This is another reason why I keep my house cleaner! What she does in three hours would take me days. Two of our bedrooms and one of the bathrooms are in our "guest wing". (It sounds bigger than it is but it is a private space.) If something breaks in your home, it's important to fix it for safety's sake and for quality of life. If you can call someone to do the job, that is ideal. We have repairmen we trust who have fixed many things in our home when necessary. Don't let things go, especially electrical or plumbing. Those two things could be tragic if something went seriously wrong.

The reason I bring up my guest wing is because I use the bedrooms for my grandchildren when they visit. The rug in one of the rooms is stained which extends in the hall because of carelessness over the years. I would love to have it replaced but that means moving lots of furniture into a smaller room and that would be challenging for us. If we replace the rug, then that means I'd probably like to repaint it and then I'd want to do the other bedroom and the hallway and the stairs and so on and so on. So when it comes to keeping your home in good shape, pick your battles. Instead of doing all that work, I bought throw rugs to cover the stains. Smart, right? The "guest wing" is not top of mind for me right now but I know I will do it someday.

We usually do a bigger project once a year. This year we repaired and repainted our barn. We asked a professional to give us a quote and hired their company since it was reasonable and their references were impeccable. That was it until next year. I'd like to keep our home in a good state so that when we decide to leave it, whether by choice or the other, it will be sellable. Painting and rugs make for a good showing but they are cheap and easier to do when the rooms are empty.

Your home is your haven so keep it nice since you will spend more time in it than anywhere else. Decorate it the way that makes you happy. Don't worry about trends and fashion. If you struggle with money, do what you can yourself but make sure you know what you are doing. Don't tackle projects that could be dangerous if you make a mistake. Better to ask a relative or friend who is an expert rather than get yourself in trouble. Be safe and enjoy your home for as long as you can.

If fixing things overwhelms you, make a list of what you would like to replace or remodel. Don't tackle them all at once but instead, create a timeline that feels comfortable to you. Your children are not waiting for an inheritance. Utilize your money wisely and enjoy what it can provide for you.

How's your vehicle doing? I drive a 2018 Toyota Camry XLE and I love it. I bought it new and paid it off last year. It has all the bells and whistles I wanted and I plan on keeping it until it dies. Robin has a 2013 Chevy Silverado which is also paid off. I love not having a car payment. In order to keep our vehicles forever, it's critical that we keep them in good shape. We get regular oil changes and if something goes wrong, we get it fixed. The tires are in good shape. Robin just got hit in a parking lot which left a dent in the driver side of his bed. It's not huge but I would still like him to get it fixed. He disagrees. Oh well, it's his truck so I will respect his wishes. I guess looks are not the most important thing. It's all about how it runs and that is perfect. I've said it before, the most important thing to keep in mind is safety, so as long as your vehicles are in good running order, you are good. And don't forget to get them inspected on time and watch that gas gauge. Fill them up when you get below a quarter tank. That's what my father taught me when I started driving.

What about your relationships? As we age and our families continue growing, it's hard to stay involved with everyone. I think that's natural but there are other vehicles to help now. Social media can be a great way to "follow" what your family is doing even when you can't be there with them to enjoy it. I use Facebook and Instagram and I review each one of them in the morning while I am enjoying my tea. I have found this especially effective with those who don't live near me. I also post on those platforms occasionally but not daily. I don't think anyone is interested in what I'm eating or thinking at every moment. One thing I have done since retiring is to reach out to at least one person daily to let them know that I am thinking about them, would like to get together with them or to thank them for having me over or enjoying time together. I have found this very effective for staying positive for myself and it makes them feel loved and thought of. This practice has become priceless! I also comment on Facebook posts when they move me or I can relate to whatever they are posting.

One thing that becomes more and more apparent as I age is that I am not the most important person in anyone's life except Robin's. My children are busy with their families and friends. My grandchildren are also very busy. My friends are mostly still working and are enjoying their growing families. Does this mean that I'm not loved? Absolutely not! Everything changes and even though you may not see or even talk to all these special people in your life all the time, it doesn't mean they don't care about you. Don't take it personally. I used to but no more. That is why I make the effort to reach out to others to let them know that I love them and that I am here when they would like to get together. I ask to see my children and my grandchildren even when I have to "make an appointment" and I'm okay with that. I'm grateful that they want to see me at all. I know that as my grandparents got older, we saw them less and less. My mom became ill in her early sixties and was bedridden so we had to go to see her. I never stopped even though it was hard and I treasure every moment I had with her. My dad was still active in our lives until his last days and my children and grandchildren still treasure their memories with him. I would like to leave that legacy with my family, too.

If there are people in your life that don't do things the way you would do them, that's okay. Mind your own business and let others live their best lives the way they want to. We are wiser from our experiences but we may not know what's best for them. When asked for advice, I share what my experience has been as exactly that, my experience but they are free to take it or leave it. If you have had a falling out with someone you genuinely care about, reach out to them and apologize. Let them know that you care about them. If they don't reciprocate, that's okay. You've said your piece and you never know what the future will hold. They may require time to think about how they feel. Life is too short to hold grudges. The time has come to leave them behind and enjoy all your relationships. It's never too late to repair one. It may just be a matter of praying for that person and letting God do the rest.

So remember, if something breaks, fix it as soon as possible. The longer you wait, the worse it gets! That goes for everything: your body, your home, your car and especially your relationships. Don't be afraid to put yourself out there and if things don't work out, don't take it personally. You've done your best and that's all you can do.

1. What are the top things in your home that require fixing? List them along with a plan on how you might go about doing that. Remember, you don't have to do them all at once. Pace yourself with a timeline that fits within your budget.

2. Do you have any relationships that you would like to fix? List those people and honestly write down how the relationship fell apart. Do you want them back in your life? Think about your end goal when it comes to making amends.

3. Now the hard part: you. What are the things that you want to fix about you? Are there habits you would like to change? It can be simple things or hard things that you know will take concentration and real change. Don't overwhelm yourself! Choose one that you would like to focus on and conquer that. Once you feel comfortable in your progress, then you can move on. Make a list with your priority at the top and write out a plan on how you will proceed. This is not a one-time activity. If your first plan doesn't work, revise it. Be flexible and kind to yourself.

Notes:

Chapter Twelve

Enjoy Your Family

Enjoy your family. Talk to them regularly. Spend time with them. Invite them over and cook for them. When they call and want to do something with you, say yes! I know it's hard to get off the couch and make that effort, but it's worth it. You are still making memories for yourself and your loved ones. It's never too late to rebuild relationships from those you've lost touch with but it does take effort.

Families are interesting. The older you get the more they change. I remember when I was younger I had two grandparents, many aunts and uncles, cousins, and of course, my parents and siblings. There were quite a few of us. Now that I'm 66, our family has leveled up. What I mean by that is all those above me (grandparents, aunts, uncles, parents) are now gone. I am at the top of the family tree! I am the oldest sibling so I have become the matriarch of my family. Robin still has an older brother but he lives out of state so it feels like he is also the top although they are the last of his siblings. So you may think, what does that mean?

Here is what it means to me. My family is so important and I would like to keep our connections strong. My brother faded away years ago when he married his second wife and they started their family. He wanted to keep it "intimate" so he declined invitations for holiday gatherings and birthday parties. He did, however, attend the big events like graduation parties, weddings and funerals. I was hurt at first but over the years, I accepted it and embraced each minute we could spend together. Those minutes mean more than they used to. Now that his daughter has married, I think he and my sister-in-law are open to spending more time with us. I'm not giving up. I continue to reach out to them and we are now going out for lunch monthly. I think knowing I have always been there for him has loosened his circle and given him the confidence to embrace our relationship again. My sister and I have always been close and I appreciate that. I value her friendship and her family.

The bottom line with family is love and understanding. We all have our own lives and priorities but there is usually that one person who is the "heart" of the family and strives to keep everyone together and connected. I am that person in my immediate family although it is challenging with the strained relationships with some individuals. I won't give up and I keep that door open just like I did with my brother. For those who choose not to engage with us, I pray for them. Some things you can't control and that's okay.

I strive to talk to my family members regularly. That doesn't mean every day but instead what feels comfortable for them and me. If I haven't talked to them in a bit, I'll text them to ensure everything is okay. That may lead to a phone conversation or a date depending on schedules. I always let them know how much I love them and that I am here when they need me. It's good to know that especially for grandchildren. You're not at the top of their "fun" list but to know that you are on their "support" list is everything.

I love cooking and it has become harder and harder to entertain as I've gotten older, but I don't want to stop. I host Thanksgiving and Easter and I love cooking both meals. One of my daughters has taken over Christmas on Christmas Eve and I'm thankful for that. Sometimes they bring part of the meal and sometimes I have it covered. If it gets too tough to make the entire meal, it's okay to ask for help. And definitely request help with the clean-up. I think you'll find that they want to be part of it and chatting over the dishes can be priceless.

I also love hosting my grandchildren whenever their schedules allow. My granddaughters, Cecelia and Eleanor are currently 11 and 9. They still enjoy sleeping over for the weekend and I have them every chance I can get. I plan a fun activity for each opportunity and I always ensure we have tasty snacks that they love. I let them relax when they want to and engage when they ask me. They know they are the "princesses" when they are with me.

I did the same for my grandsons when they were younger. Now that they are 21 and 26, they don't usually come for the weekend but Adam, the 21-year-old is still promising to come for one with his girlfriend. I welcome any opportunity with open arms. I cook their favorites when they're here. Now that Taylor, the 26-year-old is married with two children, I still love having them out for the day and dinner. I will chase their two-year-old with the biggest smile on my face because I am so grateful to have a relationship with them. It is harder the older we get, but the memories we are making are priceless. The beauty of our situation is, now that we are retired, we can rest from the big meals or the weekends with our "kids" when they go home.

I also love treating them to special events going on in our area. I will call or text them with the details and invite them to come along. I like picking up the tab to make it easier on them. Someday, they will treat me, just like my children do now.

One thing I am challenged with is gift giving. Now I know why older people give money for gifts! It's because we don't know what's "hot" anymore. I don't even understand a lot of the toys these days. Some seem stupid but the kids love them so I leave my opinions out of it. I have begun taking the girls shopping for their birthdays so they can pick out what they want. I even throw lunch in. I give them a budget and they direct me to the stores they want to shop in and we go for it. I did the same for my grandsons when they were younger. With my children and older grandchildren, I usually stick to gift cards, especially Amazon since you can buy almost anything on that site. I look for adventures that I can gift them but that can be tricky. I've tried to do some girls' weekends with my daughters and some have been a blast. Otherwise, I may schedule individual adventures since they are all so different and their schedules are tight. See, that's why older people give money! I strive to be creative and find things we can do together like theater tickets, concerts, sporting events and if you've got girls, retreats are fun and intimate.

The last topic about families that I wanted to touch on is relationships that have been lost. I have two stepchildren that are not currently in our lives. The one has been gone for many years. He lived with us when we first got married and it was a real struggle, for me especially. When he moved out, he did it in anger. I have tried over the years to reach out and repair our relationship but he was not interested in it at all. So I have only seen his children once and they probably don't even know who we are. It makes me sad but there is nothing more I can do about it. I pray for them and hope someday his children might get curious and reach out to meet us on their own, but that is a stretch. My stepdaughter is a different story. Her estrangement is more recent, only a few years. She decided she no longer wanted any relationship with us and we don't know why. I have reached out to her a number of times and sometimes she is receptive and sometimes resistant. I never know what I'm going to get. I know she struggles so on her last birthday, I sent her a text apologizing for hurting her and letting her know that I loved her and would be here when she wants to come back into the family. She did send "thank you" which is better than "f%ck you" so I took it as a win. I will continue to reach out to her gently but she may never come back. These two make me sad but I know I am doing my best and that's all any of us can do.

With other relatives that I have lost touch with, I do continue to reach out to them on Facebook. Reality tells me that we can't see everyone all the time but I do extend the invitation and every once in a while, we are able to get together. When we do, it's as if we were never apart. Enjoy all these loving relationships whenever you can. I also send Christmas cards every year with my "famous" Christmas letter to catch people up on what we have been doing the previous year and to invite them to come out to visit us if they can.

Stay open and welcoming! Families can be difficult but they can also be your lifeblood. Anytime you can spend with them is a memory in the making and will be treasured by everyone involved. I love thinking about all the wonderful times I have had and continue to have with my loved ones and I hope you do, too.

1. Think about your relationships with your family that are close and loving. Write a little bit about each one and think fondly about your part in it. Is there anything else you would like to try with them? If so, list it.

2. Think about members of your family or friends that you would like to reconnect with. List them and consider the ways you might do that and then do it!

Notes:

Chapter Thirteen

Stay Connected to Your Friends and Make New Ones

Old friends, new friends, they are all important. A strong social network is not only the key to long life but also the key to making it a joyful one. Reach out to friends regularly and make plans to do fun things together. Remember the old song "Make new friends, but keep the old, one is silver and the other gold"? What do you think that means? I could be wrong but to me, it means that friends come in all shapes and sizes. Some will be with you throughout your life and some for only a short time. Some will be very close and know all your secrets and others will be more for fun. They are all precious!

Friendships change and evolve throughout the years, don't they? When you are very young, it's all about fun. Playing and hanging out are a joy in itself. As some of us married, new friendships were created around "couple stuff" and some of our single friends were left behind until they found a partner. Once we had children, friendships changed again and it was all about the kids and their activities. When the children grew up and moved out, it was back to couple stuff. The cycle of life is wonderful but can also be difficult. As I have gotten older, I have learned an important lesson. Our happiness is truly up to us and so is our social life.

So throughout all these phases of life, some of your friends have stayed with you and that is a wonderful gift. Treasure those relationships above all because you can't replace history. I have friends that I have known for so long and we have been through many things together. Our memories are priceless.

Now that we are older, it's important to enjoy the company of friends who have the same interests and capabilities. Robin can no longer do very physical things so we have been excluded from physical activities with our couple friends who still enjoy bike riding, kayaking and hiking. I stopped drinking alcohol regularly so we are also excluded from "drinking" activities. At first, I felt hurt and shunned but now, I feel differently about it. We all go through phases and our goals and interests change. Our friends are used to my abstinence from alcohol so we do different things together from what we used to do and we still have fun and enjoy each other's company. I no longer enjoy staying up till all hours of the night for any reason. Robin is reluctant to go to many places because of his limitations. I became frustrated by these situations but then I discovered the key to the future for me: acceptance and openness to new things.

Once I retired and dove deeper into the things I enjoy doing, I began discovering new things that were available and I started inviting my friends to those. Instead of waiting for invitations to come my way, I proactively reached out to the people I wanted to spend time with and invited them to our home or to events going on around our community. Did they always say yes? Nope but I didn't take it personally. I kept inviting them until they were able to join us. I text them to just say hello. I call them to check in. I let them know how important they are to me. Do we get to hang out as much as we used to? Nope. We all have children and grandchildren that keep us busy and we prioritize family, but we do treasure the time we spend together as friends, even though it's more spread out than it used to be. As our friends retire, one by one, I'm hoping we'll be able to do more things during the week, but who knows. They are so important to me and I am willing to adapt to our future.

The key with old friends is patience, understanding and love. If you are not invited to a group activity, don't take it personally. Don't assume all your friends are out there having fun without you. But if there is something you would like to do, reach out and invite them. All things change and my lifestyle and interests are at the top of the list. Just because I don't want to do certain things anymore (or can't in Robin's case) doesn't mean I don't still love my friends. Don't just assume nobody likes you anymore and hide out at home all the time. I think you may be surprised how they really feel....maybe just like you. Friends are too precious to let them just drift away.

What about new friends? Do you think you're "too old" to make new friends? Absolutely not! Here's another benefit of retirement: your days will be filled with different activities than when you were working. All those new things that you have added to your life now give you the opportunity to meet new people. When I first started going to the YMCA, Robin went with me. He quickly faded but that didn't stop me from continuing to go and work out. I began by smiling at the other participants when I walked in to get my equipment and find my spot. Soon I felt compelled to introduce myself to those next to me. Then I spread that practice to those around me. I would chat before and after class with a few of the ladies and introduce them to each other if they didn't already know each other. Now when I go to these classes, I look forward to seeing these other amazing folks who are dedicated to taking care of themselves physically and mentally. Seeing and caring for them keeps me going consistently and brightens my life.

Another way I have made new friends is by joining the book club at my local library. Not only do I get to read books that have been loved by others, I also get to meet other women in my community. We have created relationships around our love of reading. If I see them out in public, I'm comfortable going up to them, reintroducing myself and how we know each other and chatting with them. I usually let them know how much I miss seeing them if they've missed a meeting or two or how I look forward to seeing them at our next meeting. They appreciate my kind words and I appreciate them!

Church is another great way to meet new people. During the service its rather difficult but if you go to any of the "other" activities within the church, I have found people welcoming. This is so important since I normally go alone. Think about that when you see someone come in alone to a group that you might already be comfortable in. Smile and welcome them. Introduce yourself.

So what are some of the new groups that you have begun attending where you might make new friendships? I made new friends at my artist circle, the water aerobics class I attended and pretty much any other new group I've added. Here is another bit of advice: if you see someone that you believe you know but you can't remember their name, don't let that cause you to shy away from saying hello. If you find yourself in that situation, walk up and say, hi, I'm Susan from book club or whatever the case may be. Usually when you say your name first, not only does it allow them to connect the dots as to how they might know you, but they may also say their name. If they don't, it's okay to ask. I usually say, I'm sorry I've forgotten your name and then they offer it. You should not be afraid to approach them. We are all just people looking for connections in this life. Be the conduit!

Don't be afraid to invite others to the activities you enjoy either, especially if they are newly retired. They may be looking for guidance and they may not be. Respect their boundaries. If you see that they are really interested in an experience you've had or a group you are in, that is the perfect time to extend the invitation.

1. Think about the friendships you have today. List each of your friends and write a little "story" about them. How long have you known them? Where did you meet? What are some of the most fun things you've done together? What do you love the most about them?

2. Next, think about some of the new people you may have met now that you are retired. Are there any that come to mind that you might want to get to know better? What next step are you willing to take to do that?

3. Are you feeling like you could use another friend or two? Think of ways in your community where you might be able to do that. List them and write out a simple plan on how to go about it. Don't over complicate it.

Notes:

Chapter Fourteen

Don't Let Yourself Go!

You are still a priority! Get your hair done professionally in a style that makes you feel good about yourself. Use beauty products that are non-toxic and take good care of your skin. Wear makeup when you want to, again non-toxic and in a way that makes you feel beautiful. Take showers and baths regularly because you will get stinky. Wear clean clothes and wash your bedding weekly. That gets stinky, too.

Taking care of ourselves is so critical for our self-confidence and happiness. I used to think that when I retired, I would no longer get my hair colored. In so doing, my natural color would begin to take over and according to De, my daughter and hair professional, it is almost all white. I know some people think that is a beautiful look and it is for those who want it. My hair was almost black when I was younger and I have continued to keep that base color of dark brown. I am currently adding some fun colors as highlights and right now I have a vivid purple. My hair is also fairly long with bangs. I blow it dry and finish it with a straightening hair drying brush. All of these factors make me look younger than my 66 years in part. It's not just my hair but that is a big part of it. When people first see me, they don't think old lady, at least not right away. I also have my eyebrows dyed to match my hair which again, gives me a more youthful look. As a side note, De also waxes my eyebrows and upper lip to keep them shapely and clean respectively. Is your hair, eyebrows and lip important to you? Maybe, maybe not. It's all up to the individual. For me, I'm not ready to go all natural because my hair makes me feel beautiful. If your hair does the same thing, then go for it!

How about skincare? Are you a soap and water kind of gal when it comes to washing your face? Does your skin feel hydrated and smooth and does it look healthy? Great! For me, I have discovered that non-toxic beauty products work best. I use a facewash based on essential oils along with a gentle exfoliating scrub a couple times a week. I use an under-eye cream to keep the bags and crepiness away. I also use a moisturizer with an essential oil to keep my skin smooth and healthy looking. All these things are keeping the wrinkles and age spots to a minimum. I have changed how I take care of my skin over the years to adapt to my age and current circumstances, and so should you.

Makeup is another piece of our regimen that has changed over the years (hopefully!). I used to wear makeup every day, no matter what I was doing. I got this from my mom. She wore makeup even when she became bedridden in later life, including her blue eye shadow. Now that I am not working, I wear makeup only occasionally. Since I love to work out at the Y, I definitely don't wear it there. I give it my all and I sweat during almost all workouts so why would I? Now I wear makeup when it makes sense, going out with friends, volunteering at our local theater or on a date with Robin. Even when I do wear makeup, it's only to enhance my features. I used to love eye shadow and I learned from a professional how to apply it using three different colors to really give my eyes a pop. Now I stick to the basics: coverup under my eyes and on my chin, translucent powder to reduce shine, an eyelash curler and mascara, eye liner under my eyes only, blush and a neutral lipstick or lip gloss. All of this is to even out my skin tone and enhance my eyes. Since I wear glasses, that is even more important to me. Do I really need any of it? Robin says no but I enjoy going the extra mile on special occasions. It makes me feel pretty and builds my confidence. Whether you wear makeup or not, beauty still comes from within so remember the most important piece: a genuine smile. That will make your face light up and your eyes twinkle and what could be more beautiful than that?

The next topic is sensitive. Take showers and baths regularly because you will get stinky. I struggle with this because my skin is dry and bathing too often seems to dry it out even more. So here is the rule I live by: when I work outside in the summer and I sweat, I take a shower…period. I come in and strip and go directly to the shower. I use products that are non-toxic so they are gentle on my body. I wash my hair, too. The summer is particularly tricky because of the heat. Everything gets stinky when you sweat so don't fool yourself into thinking it doesn't. The winter is when you should hold off on bathing too much since your skin will be extra dry because of the cold and indoor heating. You may not be able to "smell yourself" so if someone else mentions that you are stinky, believe them. I think a good rule of thumb is to bath at least a couple times per week regularly.

I know as I was growing up, women went to the beauty parlor to get their hair done once a week. And that was the only time they washed it. These were older women and now I get it. My hair is dry too. So use good non-toxic products on your hair to keep it in good shape or hit the salon weekly to let them do it.

Make sure your private parts are clean, too. Wash them daily to avoid infections and discomfort. Now they have adult wipes to make it even easier. Use them after bowel movements to stay clean. Check those underarms and use natural deodorant to feel fresh. No one wants to talk about these things but they are important to stay healthy and confident.

Now that you have your nice clean body, it's also important to wear clean clothes! My rule of thumb is to wear it for a day and throw it in the hamper. Not only does it now smell like me, I'm sure I've spilled something on myself during the day. I don't want it to stain. Before putting your clothes on, check them for stains and rips. If you find either, throw them in the garbage. They are not even "donate worthy". Or if they are your favorite and very comfortable, save them for working outside or for doing messy projects, but they are not "going out worthy" anymore. If something doesn't fit right, donate it. If you hate it and keep passing it by in your closet, donate it. Thank your donations for their service to you and know they will find a good home with someone who will love and appreciate them. Don't wear things if they don't make you feel confident and pretty. You deserve only the best at this point in your life. Buy things that make you feel happy.

And don't forget about your bedding. You should be washing it regularly or it will stink up your home and maybe even you. I wash mine at least once a week in warmer weather and then weekly or bi-weekly during the colder months. If you have pets that sleep with you, stick to the weekly plus routine. It's not healthy to sleep in a dirty bed.

1. These are some of the things I have learned and I'm sure you have similar practices. What other things can you think of that are important to you when taking care of yourself?

2. What are practices that you currently have that you would like to maintain? Are there some that you would like to change or modify? Write down how you take care of yourself today and consider any changes that you would like to incorporate.

Notes:

Chapter Fifteen

Do Your Best
to Get Rid of Bad Habits

Now is the time to get rid of bad habits. If you smoke, stop. If you drink alcohol, know your limits. If you can't respect them like I couldn't, quit drinking. That has changed my life this year. Anything that affects your health in a negative way, reconsider it. Talk it over with your doctor if you're not sure.

Smoking isn't good for anyone. I started smoking when I was 14 years old. It was cool back then. I could buy cigarettes from a machine at the grocery store for 50 cents a pack. I snuck a cigarette while I was outside walking so my parents wouldn't see me. I only smoked once in a while and I would say it wasn't a habit at that time.

When I was 16 years old, we were having dinner at my grandparents' house. My purse was in the living room and my little sister who was 7 years old at the time was snooping in my purse and found my pack of cigarettes. She waltzed into the dining room to announce it holding them high. I thought I would get into trouble but since both of my parents smoked, they accepted in without a thought. My mother let me know that I could smoke in the house if I wanted to and requested I not hide it in my bedroom because of fire hazards. I was shocked! So began my true habit of smoking since I could now smoke whenever I wanted to. They still didn't appreciate us smoking in the bathrooms at school but I never got caught and suspended.

Later that year, I had surgery for a pilonidal cyst. I was in the hospital for five days and I didn't smoke there. When I returned home and settled into bed, one of the first things my mother brought to me was a pack of her cigarettes which were Larks with a charcoal filter (yuck), an ashtray and a pack of matches. Since I had not smoked for five days, I let her know that I thought I was interested in quitting. She insisted that I not and that having a cigarette would make me feel better. I remember the first few tasting terrible but I continued on. As soon as I was able, I grabbed a pack of my dad's cigarettes which were Winston's and I grew to love them. I experimented with different brands throughout my smoking career but I always smoked name brands.

I had two children and talked to my gynecologist about smoking. He told me I shouldn't quit while I was pregnant since it would upset the baby, so I didn't. I even remember smoking when I was nursing once the babies came home. This was in the 1980's and it was a different time. We all smoked everywhere, in our homes, in places of work, even in airplanes! Restaurants and bars were a given since everyone loved smoking after a meal or while they were having a cocktail. And you bet we smoked in the car with our babies in the back. When I think of how crazy that was now, I am sorry that I was a smoker. I did try to quit a few times throughout my life and was never successful until I turned 39.

When I was 39 that marked 25 years of smoking. Smoking was becoming more and more taboo. You couldn't smoke in airplanes anymore and I traveled for a living. You couldn't smoke at work anymore so I had to step outside to have one and there were many times, I would stand there smoking in a blizzard. When I finally made the decision to quit for good at 39, it was in February. I reminded myself of all the reasons I no longer wanted to smoke: it was expensive, it made my clothes smell, it made my body and hair smell, it made my breath unbearable, it was no longer relaxing but instead a hassle. When I couldn't have a cigarette for an extended period of time, it made me anxious. It was dirty and I had to clean my house regularly to get the yellow tar and nicotine off my pictures, walls, etc.

Since I was so serious about it this time, I announced it to everyone: my coworkers, my family, my friends, anyone who I encountered. I did it cold turkey and it was one of the hardest things I had ever done in my life. I was a true addict. I was grouchy and I snipped at others for a couple of weeks. I lost ten pounds in the first year because I walked and walked and walked to get rid of my desire to smoke. I changed all my "smoking habits" to new ones. Robin even bought me cigarettes and begged me to start smoking again because I was so difficult to live with. But I threw them in the trash can and declared I would never smoke again.....and I didn't. It was one of the most beneficial things I could have done for myself and my family. Both of my parents died from COPD even though they quit later in life; my mom died at 72 and my dad died at 86. I hope I will be spared that disease. I have done all I can to help myself.

I am so grateful that I have been cigarette free for 27 years. I can breathe well and I am healthy. I love working out as you know and not smoking has enabled me to do cardio. So if you are still smoking, I would encourage you to stop immediately. I know you must love it or are an addict like I was if you are still smoking since it is so inconvenient to truly enjoy it. If quitting cold turkey is too much for you to think about, then talk to your doctor or join a "quit smoking" program, whatever will work for you. The freedom and health you will receive is priceless and hey, you will also save a boatload of money, too. Your family will be so proud of you and you will be proud of yourself. There is no downside, so make up your mind and get it done today. I believe in you. If I could do it so can you!

Now onto the socially accepted and encouraged practice of drinking alcohol. I have had a very wonderful and tumultuous relationship with alcohol. I started drinking when I was 17, probably late for some of you.

I remember going to my boyfriend's house and his parents had a bar in their basement. They fed me drink after drink and I had never had alcohol before. Needless to say, I got so drunk I couldn't drive home and I barely knew where I was! I slept in a spare room, I think and I vomited all night, all over myself, the bed and even the walls. I got up and slithered out the door. Boy, was his mom mad when she found the mess. Our relationship ended soon after and my shame went with me.

That began my journey with alcohol. I found many different drinks throughout my drinking career from Tequila sunrises to beer to whatever my friends were drinking and found a love of White Russians, an alcohol milkshake. I went through times of sobriety in my life when I was pregnant and my children were small but I kept coming back to alcohol when it was socially encouraged to share a cocktail. Isn't it the best way to join a group? We share laughs and stories, we dance, we play games or watch sports and we drink.

Next I found my love for wine and 19 years ago, we moved to a small town on the Niagara wine trail. Not only is it a beautiful place, it's perfect for growing grapes (and other produce used in making wine but mostly grapes). We would go on the wine trails for Mother's Day, Sunday Fun Days and any other day we felt like it. I became a member of one of the wineries. This "encouraged" me to pick up a case of their wine twice a year. I started by drinking the sweeter, fruitier wines but as my palate matured, I moved to the deep delicious reds. They were magical and powerful.

The ladies I worked with at the end of my career introduced me to Caymus, an amazing cabernet sauvignon from Napa Valley. When we opened a bottle, it was only the beginning. Bottle after bottle came and went and I embraced it's amazing taste and effects. When I retired, I ordered a case of it as a thank you from the company, so it was readily available to me whenever I wanted it.

During my first summer of retirement, I found myself too much in love with robust cabernet sauvignons and I got hammered on a few occasions. I felt shame and weakness at not being able to control my drinking. On the last occasion where I had drunk too much Caymus and spent hours in the bathroom throwing up, I knew that I didn't want to be that person anymore. I came down the next morning, painfully hung over and declared to Robin, "I think it's time for me to break up with red wine. I love it too much." And guess what? He agreed! This really shocked me. He did say that I should drink something that I don't like as much and it got me to thinking. I spent the next few days questioning myself and my relationship with alcohol. Was I an alcoholic? I didn't drink every day and I didn't always get drunk, but I knew that my drinking was no longer serving me. I thought it was time to "take a break".

    I stopped drinking for about a year and a half. Was it hard? Not to physically stop drinking but the social aspect was harder than I thought it would be. What do I mean by that? Well, drinking alcohol is part of being social, right? All our friends drink, most of our family drinks and most of the things we used to do centered around drinking. Going out to dinner, to the theater, parties, playing cards were all different because I no longer drank. It made others almost uncomfortable to have me around. Our activities together changed or stopped. No more going out on the wine trail. The social changes were the hardest part, especially at first.

    Now that I am eighteen months into sobriety, I am feeling much more relaxed with my choice. Will I ever have another drink? I did on a vacation with friends. I made the decision to have a couple of mudslides in the afternoon around the pool and a White Russian in the evening after dinner. When I came home, I went back to sobriety. I had another White Russian on our anniversary when Robin and I went out for dinner. I'm lucky since I am not an alcoholic but I still do not want alcohol to be a regular part of my life. I guess I'm thinking of it more as a treat. Will I drink on every vacation or expand my "treats"? I'm not planning on it but we'll see what the future holds. What I love about being sober is my excellent sleep, my clear head, my caloric savings, never having to worry about "driving legally drunk" and not embarrassing myself, just to name a few. It has changed my life and I'm not giving that up.

Alcohol is fun, delicious and social but it is also not "good" for us. Having a glass of wine with dinner or a couple when you go out is okay but not on the regular. I won't go into all the negative effects because you can look them up on the internet, but for me, it no longer served me. Just like with smoking, I am not confident that if I have a glass of wine occasionally that I won't go down the road I got off of a year ago since that particular drink was my downfall. So, this is what I'll leave you with when it comes to alcohol: if you feel comfortable with your intake and it has not affected you or your health negatively, enjoy it. If not, now may be the time to "take a break" and see how different you feel without the shame and physical affects you may have experienced in the past. Life is still beautiful and fun without it.

The last bad habit I'd like to talk about is "beating yourself up". This can be something that becomes more frequent as we age. It can be physical and emotional. I have already talked about how important it is to take care of our bodies. I have learned to pace myself when doing physical projects. I have added "relaxation time" to my daily schedule. I want to continue to challenge myself to stay strong and active. There are times when I push too hard. I must add in recovery time and sometimes even take aspirin the next day to rejuvenate my body. While I enjoy pushing myself, I am still careful. I think that may be the key. I watch where I am going and when I become too weary while doing anything, I take a five-minute break. I have broken my wrist, my nose and my ankle when I was not being careful so I have learned that lesson deeply. I know there are people in their 70's, 80's and 90's that are still running races and doing strength training that is beyond me. You may be one of them. But I know my limits and I continue to challenge them gradually and I think that is the key. Don't beat your body up attempting to do something that you have not prepared for. Be logical.

Equally important is not beating yourself up emotionally. What I mean by that is STOP BEING SO CRITICAL OF YOU! I remember when my mom was very sick and I went over to my parents' house to help out. My dad, who was in his 80's was still taking care of her every day. They lived in a split-level home and my mom was bedridden in an upstairs bedroom. He ran up and down those stairs a hundred times a week to cater to her every requirement. He never complained and I thought he was superman.

When I was there sleeping on the couch in the living room, I heard him get up while it was still dark. He came downstairs, went into the kitchen and started his routine. He was talking to himself and he said so many horrible things about how stupid he was, how clumsy he was, how forgetful he was and how he just wasn't good enough. It was 5:30 a.m. and he had set his alarm to begin caring for my mother. Tears filled my eyes and after I collected myself, I went into the kitchen. I put my arm around him and told him how amazing he was and how much I loved him. He looked at me as if I was speaking a foreign language and I think to him, I was.

How often do you find yourself talking to yourself about the same things? I know I do. I would never say those things to anyone else (except in anger and I still wish I wouldn't!) so why do we go there so quickly with ourselves? Mel Robbins wrote a book about the "High Five Habit" where she recommends you give yourself a high five in the mirror each morning when you wake up. She instructs you to look into your eyes and wish yourself a great day and know that you are doing your best and that is pretty darn good. What a novel idea. Every time I stumble, I tell myself not to be so clumsy. Every time I drop something, I tell myself to watch what I am doing. Every time I make a mistake, I call myself stupid.

I am still working on this bad habit not only with myself but with Robin as well. I would like to stop being so critical of him and me. Because this habit is so ingrained in my psyche, I would like to try making amends right away when I take this negative route. If I say something to myself, I will apologize and confirm that I am doing my best and that is enough. If I say something negative to Robin or anyone else, if I didn't really mean it (or even if I did in a moment of anger), I will apologize for overstepping and let him / them know how much they mean to me, or how I really feel about the situation. One way to prevent this from occurring so often is to follow the rule my mom told me so long ago: "If you can't say something nice, don't say anything at all." You can think it but if it's about you, it will still hurt. How about if we say nice things to ourselves and others throughout the day to lift us all up?

-

These were my top three bad habits that I have already corrected or are currently working on. What comes to mind for you when you think about things you'd like to change that may be harming you in some way? Write them down and give them a good think. Are you ready to make positive changes? What would that mean? Write down as many as you can think of but don't tackle them all at once. Which one might you want to prioritize? Start there.

-
-
-
-
-
-
-
-

Notes:

Chapter Sixteen

Drink Tons of Water

Drinks are an interesting topic for seniors. One thing that I have found universally is that most seniors limit their intake of beverages to avoid having to go to the bathroom. Don't do that! Your intake of liquids and the release of what you don't need via urinating is essential to our survival. (It also helps with pooping.) And water should be at the top of your list.

I have a pretty limited menu of liquids on a daily basis. I start by drinking a glass of water (about 12 oz.) followed by a glass of celery juice. You might be wondering why celery juice and where do you even get it? I discovered this gem years ago when I broke my ankle. In attempting to enhance my recovery, my daughter, De brought over her juicer and created different fresh juices for me to drink during the day. My recovery was incredible and I attribute it to my excellent care from my orthopedic surgeon and my family. Everyone provided me with healthy drinks and food and I did better than expected. They cared for me in such a loving way. I decided to get a juicer of my own so I could continue this practice and focused on celery juice because of its overall benefits. We buy bunches of celery when I run out and Robin kindly juices it for me, storing it in a pitcher for easy access. I love it.

After my celery juice, I move onto tea. My favorite morning cup is Red Rose and I typically have three of them with whole milk. I absolutely love it! After my second cup, I make my breakfast and take my vitamin supplements with a glass of water. I continue drinking water all day, refilling my 12 oz. glass from the spigot in my refrigerator that provides cold filtered water. No plastic bottles for me.

In the afternoon, I usually have another cup of tea, right now it's Irish Breakfast for a mid-afternoon break and another tea in the evening before going to bed. My nighttime tea is usually an herbal tea so that it doesn't keep me up at night but honestly, even when I drink a black tea, I usually sleep like a baby.

So that is my menu of drinks on a daily basis. I don't care for soda pop except for the occasional ginger ale if I'm feeling like a need a sugary drink, but we don't buy it. All of my other drinks are enjoyed when I go out. I love coffee as a treat especially in a really good restaurant. I might try other things like mocktails or alcohol-free beer, but normally when I'm out, I just drink water with a lemon in it. Water, water, water! And yes, I am in the bathroom quite a bit but I also know when not to load up on liquids like before going to a movie or live theater or if I am in any place where a bathroom is not readily available. Normally, I keep water on hand and enjoy it throughout the day.

So, why is what you drink so important? Because they all have their own health benefits (or not). Rather than list them all here since I'm not a doctor, I challenge you to look them up on the internet, read the labels on packages or bottles or talk to the vendors selling them to understand more. The "Medical Medium" is where I learned about the benefits of celery juice. I don't buy processed juices at the grocery store. If you would like to make your own from fresh fruits and vegetables, I applaud you. Buying a good juicer is absolutely worth it if you love juices. If you do choose to buy them from a store, ensure they are filled with nutrients and not sugar or chemicals.

Here are a few reasons why I drink water. Our bodies are mostly water and we can only live a few days without it. That should be incentive enough, but some of the other benefits are: flushing your organs, keeping your skin moisturized, keeping your veins and blood flowing and just staying hydrated overall. Do you know that when you're hungry and you don't want to eat at that moment, having a glass of water can dispel your hunger pains? Also, if you get a headache, try drinking a glass of water before taking aspirin. With both of these issues, you may just be dehydrated. I also sweat a lot. Whenever I exert myself with exercise, garden work or even just when it's hot outside, I will start sweating. My face gets red and it pours down my face. Is this a good thing? I'm not sure, but I do know when it's happening, it's even more important for me to rehydrate with a full glass of water. I think staying hydrated even helps me sleep better.

As I said, I'm not a doctor. I'm just a lover of life and I am focused on staying healthy and active. The internet has many wonderful reasons to drink water and guidance on other liquids that are healthy. Find what makes you feel good and look good every single day. If something is not doing that, consider eliminating it and find something else. Be creative but stay away from sugary drinks that have no health benefit. It's okay to "treat yourself" every once in a while but strive to make your main source of fluids water.

So what are you drinking regularly now? What changes might you want to make to try to improve this aspect of your health? List them and get started.

-
-
-
-
-
-
-
-
-

Notes:

Chapter Seventeen

Have Fun!

You have more days behind you than ahead of you but your life is not over. Laugh daily! Find what gives you joy and immerse yourself in it. Never stop learning or exploring. You are on a never ending "summer vacation" just like when you were a kid. Act like one! Surround yourself with things you love. Rescue a dog or cat. They will love you unconditionally and you will be making a difference in the world. Just make sure you are committed to the responsibility for them for the rest of their lives. Have faith in a higher power that has your back. Believe that you are not alone because you're not. Don't worry about stuff that you have no control over. Give it to God and let "him" figure it out. Pray for others with all your heart. Wake up each day knowing you are loved!

I heard my friend, Lynette say once the statement that having more days behind her than ahead of her played into the decisions she made about her future. At the time, the statement terrified me. To say that I am on "my final chapter" seemed so dark, but is it? I think the true power of that statement is that we can no longer afford to waste time. So every day, I spend my time doing things I enjoy, even "work". When I am weeding my gardens, I thank God for the physical ability to do it. I relish the grounding

I feel when I am trimming the dead flowers off my bushes and removing weeds that have the potential to choke the plants I wish to gaze upon. I look at the results of my sweat and see the beauty in what God and I have sculpted together. I watch as the hummingbirds and bees drink their life-giving nectar. What an amazing gift! Not to mention the Vitamin D I am absorbing while in the sunshine. So, find pleasure in everything you do, even the perceived "mundane" tasks.

Physical strength and mobility may not be permanent so it is critical to maintain it through exercise and healthy foods, but to also do the most difficult things on your bucket list first. Do you want to take a hiking vacation to Ireland? How about a horseback riding adventure in Montana? Don't wait until you can't participate in all the activities involved. Do those types of things first.

It's time for you to fulfill your dreams. When my mom was in the nursing home at the end of her life, she wanted to go home to open a bakery. We had a separate entrance to our home because it was once owned by a dentist and she had always envisioned having a little bakery in it, filled with her homemade pies, cakes and cookies. Her face lit up every time she talked about it. It was as if she really believed she could do it, even though it was now physically impossible.

In the last weeks of my dad's life, he talked about moving back to England to live with his little brother, Pat. My mom was gone and so was Uncle Pat's wife and he really believed they could take care of each other. They were both in their 80's! When my dad immigrated to the U.S. from England in the 1950's, he longed for his home, but once he met my mother, he acclimated to being an American and became a citizen. He never visited his family or his homeland because my mom never wanted to. But at the end of his life, he longed to return. It broke my heart. Why didn't I take him after my mom passed away? I wish I had.

1. Don't wait until it's too late to do those things that you have always dreamed of. The time is now! It may be something that isn't even on your bucket list or it may be at the top. Have a good think about it in a quiet place, without distractions. Make a list of the things that come to mind and then start planning them, one by one. Start with the one that is most difficult or the one you are the most passionate about. Can you even remember how to have fun? Bring back the child in you and list the things that make you happy, small and big things.

Notes:

Chapter Eighteen

Laugh Daily!

Keep laughter in your life. When I thought about that action, I thought is it too much to suggest we should find things in life funny on a daily basis? First of all, life is hard and as I've gotten older, it gets even harder. We don't look the same, we don't feel the same, we don't do the same things every day that we've done in our past. But can we still have fun? Absolutely!

Instead of getting caught up in the news and disheartening conspiracy theories, find humor in the simple things, especially yourself. My teeth and my smile are not as perfect as they used to be. So what. My children pointed out to me that I have changed my smile to hide my imperfect teeth and it looks kind of goofy. Just be me and give that big warm smile that you are known for Susan. So I started doing that again and you know what? I like my pictures better now.

I've noticed that Robin doesn't laugh anymore except when he is watching Seinfeld. I thought, why do you keep watching that old show? You've seen those episodes a million times. And you know what? He still finds them hilarious. Who am I to tell him what to enjoy? I love silly animal videos so I watch them and smile. If I find myself laughing, I share the video.

How about when you've watching your own pets? You know they are just as funny if not more humorous than the ones online. And don't even get me started on my grandchildren and great grandchildren. Not only do they do funny things but they warm my heart with gratitude and love as I laugh with them.

Lastly, don't forget to laugh at yourself. Just this morning I dropped the tea cannister while I was attempting to put it back on the counter and fumbled it before it hit the ground, scared my dogs and tea bags when flying. Fortunately, it's made out of tin so nothing was really damaged, but instead of beating myself up for being clumsy, I chuckled and put everything back. I do pretty silly things on a daily basis, even in public and instead of getting embarrassed, I laugh, maybe make a little joke and allow others to laugh with me.

When something really strikes me as funny, I let it go. I've seen people stifle their laugh but not me. There have been times when it has brought me to tears and my stomach is sore but boy, is it worth it! Just let it go and who knows, others may just follow along with you.

1. What are your favorite things that make you laugh? Make a list and be sure to add more of them to your life!

-
-
-
-
-
-
-
-
-
-
-
-
-

Notes:

Chapter Nineteen

You Can Still Feel Joy!

Find what gives you joy and immerse yourself in it. Do you even know what gives you joy? When I retired, I thought about that on the retreat I went to on my last day of work. I had spent so much time deep in my career, raising my family and keeping up with my house, that I had lost sight of what gives me true pleasure. Retirement has given me back the precious commodity of time to not only think about what gives me joy, but to actually pursue it.

While I was working, I read many things and heard many comments about utilizing 15 minutes a day to pursue your bliss because it would add up. It sounds good as a theory, but the reality for me was that I couldn't even calm my mind in 15 minutes to start something. Now I can dedicate a whole afternoon or even a whole day to something I love.

I found that going back in my mind to childhood to list some of the things that gave me so much joy really helped.

- I no longer feel guilty if I choose to spend an afternoon reading a book.
- Now I love making complicated recipes to challenge myself and serve something really special, whether it's for just me and Robin or

- to larger groups when we are entertaining.
- I have created space for my art supplies in our family room for easy accessibility to them and now I can jump in and out of a project when I feel like it. Not having to set up and clean up every time has been priceless.
- I also love decorating for different holidays. Instead of having to rush through it, I can now take my time and create new groupings and even change them if I don't like my first attempt.
- And I know you probably will think I'm crazy, but I also love cleaning and especially cleaning things out. I'm not talking about routine cleaning. I have an amazing cleaner that does that for me. I'm talking about cleaning closets, shelves, drawers, outside spaces like our barn and garage, things like that. Not only can I take my time and do a really good job with it, but once I've found things I no longer need, I give them away to others who will enjoy them. This gives me joy in so many different ways.
- I also love my home and redecorating it when the mood strikes me. I enjoy thinking it through and then putting the pieces into action. I know that I may get to the point where it won't matter as much, but I still love change and creating something new in my safe haven.

1. What are some of the things you have put to the side while you were adulting in so many ways? Have a think about it and start listing them here. What might you have to do to reinstate that activity? Add any preparation necessary to get started. And remember, going back to your childhood is a worthwhile start to get the juices flowing.

Notes:

Chapter Twenty

Never Stop Learning Or Exploring

We are never too old to learn new things. This can tie in very nicely to what brings you joy. There may be new things that you don't even know about yet that can bring you happiness.

When it comes to learning, I don't ever want to stop. There are so many free opportunities in my community all the time and when I see them and my calendar is free, I sign up. From nutrition to crafts to painting to gardening, whatever, I am there! What about friends who might have a skill that you don't? You might ask them to teach and mentor you. They will appreciate your interest and you will have an opportunity to add to your knowledge as well as deepening your relationship with them.

I never want to feel like I know everything. I love trivia and I answer questions daily. I love word games and I play them daily. I love listening to friends, family and strangers to learn from them. I offer opinions only when asked. I enjoy listening to hear others' points of view. I read teaching books in addition to pleasure books.

My sister wants to go to college when she retires to get the much-coveted degree she never had. Maybe you'll want to go all in like her. Whatever it is, it's not beyond your reach if you really want it. Learn and explore all you can while you can. Don't waste this opportunity.

The world is a big place and you can dig deeper into the areas around you and branch out from there. I try never to pass up an invitation to travel and neither should you, especially if you've never been to that destination before. I thought it might be fun to alternate between places in the U.S. which is where I live and abroad. I'm not sure how far I'll get but I love seeing new things, especially when it's related to history. Maybe you can even dabble into learning a new language to prepare.

Exploring is more than just traveling though. Exploring is digging deeper into something or somewhere. Maybe it's a local park or hiking trail or learning more about Italy. Don't think of it just from a sightseer's perspective, but if an area spikes your interest, think of it as an explorer might, asking questions and taking a more introspective look. You don't even have to go anywhere to do it. You can do it in a book or from your computer.

1. What are your top desires when it comes to learning something new? This should be an organic list. Start with one or two that you are passionate about. Don't forget to list how you might learn these things: a book, a class, a mentor, a facility?

2. Are there different things or places you'd like to explore? List those and how you might want to pursue them. Keep it fun and light. Even if you never pursue them, it's still fun thinking about them, right?

Notes:

Chapter Twenty-One

Embrace Your Never-Ending Vacation

You are on a never ending "summer vacation" just like when you were a kid. Act like one! When I see older people walking around with their heads bent and plodding through life, it makes me sad. Just because we have more years behind us than ahead of us, doesn't mean we can't have fun and be silly.

We really do have a "never ending vacation" since we don't have the obligation of a work schedule so take advantage of it. I have talked about how much I love sitting on my porch for hours, drinking tea and enjoying nature, a beautiful breeze and my amazing property. I don't have to fill my days with chores just to feel productive. If I choose to spend an afternoon reading a book, that is perfect.

One of my fondest memories of my dad was when I took him grocery shopping. He pushed the cart and I grabbed our goodies. He was looking at something and I called to him to catch up with me. Instead of plodding along pushing the cart, he instead took a quick trot, jumped on the back of the cart and slid over to me with the biggest smile on his face. Would many 84-year-olds do that? No, but a kid would.

Think about your summer vacations as a child and what made you so happy on them. I know I enjoyed reading, writing stories, riding my bike, swimming and spending time with friends. Now I'm doing all those types of activities again and with no time pressures. When I go to the YMCA, I love classes and I love being silly (but safe) in them. There are times when I can't follow the instructor and go rogue with my own moves, laughing constantly. I continue to introduce myself to new people. When I walk into the class, I smile and wave at everyone and they warmly smile and wave back. After the classes, I let them know what a great job they did. We are not all equal in our strength and abilities, but we are all doing our best and that is what kids do.

Even in the winter, I continue to look for fun things to do. Craft classes and fun lectures remind me of the day camps I went to as a child. Whatever the outcome of my project, I embrace my creativity and applaud my courage to try something new, while laughing at myself and with others as we all learn together.

How about exploring things in your area like museums, the zoo, botanical gardens, art galleries, etc. My dad used to take us on an outing every weekend when we were children. We got to know the above mentioned so well that we would dart to our favorite exhibits to admire them again. You can do these field trips alone or with a friend who might also enjoy them. Take your time really exploring each display and don't be afraid to talk to the other patrons about what you find. You know children would. It's more fun sharing thoughts and ideas and you never know what you might learn.

I love doing projects with my grandchildren and watching them as they blissfully create something special. I dance without caring who's watching and nothing makes me happier than seeing others join in with joy and love.

In my volunteer activities, I encourage others to have fun with whatever job they are given and bring joy to those they serve. If there are things that I don't enjoy, I don't do them anymore. We have that choice.

1. So have fun and remember you don't have to cram everything into the weekends anymore. You have your whole life to do whatever you want. Take some time to think about your past summer vacations. What were your favorite activities? List them here.

-
-
-
-
-
-
-
-
-

2. Once you are done with your list (and take the time to remember those happy times thoroughly), think about how you might bring them back into your life now. Start with your favorite and come up with a plan to incorporate it. Need to buy equipment? Do it. Would you love a class to refresh your skills or learn a new one? Look for one. Ask friends to do it with you or if you choose to try it alone, make new friends. Don't rush through this. Embrace it.

Notes:

Chapter Twenty-Two

Surround Yourself With Things You Love

Throughout the years, I have learned more and more about interior decorating. I have enjoyed hanging wallpaper, picking out just the right furniture, pictures, flooring, etc. I'm sure you have as well. Now it's all about enjoying my home, inside and out, with things that make me happy. Will my house be in Better Homes and Gardens? Maybe but also maybe not.

What I've learned is that I really enjoy displaying things that I have created, hanging pictures of my family and friends and buying things that attract my attention at estate sales, yard sales, wherever they might strike my fancy. I have an art / craft center in my family room. My living room is filled with toys for my great-granddaughters. I have birds and angels throughout my house. Does it all look perfectly coordinated? Probably not, but it makes me happy to look at it all.

One thing I have learned over the years is not to display rare or expensive things. That's one of the reasons I love shopping at estate and yard sales. When children are around, anything can happen and I don't want to get upset if something breaks. It might even be me that breaks it. They are only things and I always joke with my children that when I die, they will probably sell all my things for $.25 each. And if they do, that's okay since I won't be around to fret about it.

I still love decorating for the different holidays and seasons even though it may not be seen by many others. It makes me happy and that's all that matters. Enjoy your home!

1. Take some time to list some of the things that make you happy and content in your home. When you are listing them out, take a few minutes to remember where you got them and why they mean so much to you. Reminiscing about your mementos is one of the reasons to keep them around.

2. Is there anything in your home that you don't enjoy anymore? This could be a gift that someone gave you or something that you bought yourself. Maybe it's time to let it go? Make a list below of the things that no longer serve you. Consider how you might pass them along and do it. Thank them for their service and know that they can now enhance someone else's life.

Notes:

Chapter Twenty-Three

Rescue a Dog or Cat

Who's greeting you when you come home? Need a snuggle partner? Rescuing an "unwanted" animal may be just what is missing from your life. They will love you unconditionally and you will be making a difference in the world. I am 66 years old and we have a five-year-old pit / lab mix and a nine-year-old golden retriever. There are some days when I would like to be left alone but then I look at their faces and feel so grateful to have them both in our lives.

Daisy, the golden retriever, we bought from an older couple in our town who had purchased two siblings as puppies. The man was bedridden and his wife thought they would be good company for him. As you can imagine, they were active puppies and too much for them and their serenity. We were excited to take one as a companion to our Aussie / lab mix at home, Chubbs. When our beloved Chubbs died at 16, Daisy was so lonely and depressed that we began looking for a rescue to join her. We found Bella, the lab / pit mix and it was instant love for Daisy and Robin. They are still together today and still as close as ever.

If you already have pets, that is wonderful. As we get older, some of us can't handle bigger dogs and very work intensive puppies. But how about adopting an older dog? Or a lap cat? When you rescue an animal, you receive unconditional love and companionship. But make a good choice. When Daisy passes away, I was thinking maybe a lap dog might be more practical or even a cat. Whatever we decide, I know it will be a decision made with love.

You may live in a place that doesn't allow pets. Maybe you could visit your local shelter to help out. I know they offer their animals for afternoon dates and that dog will be so grateful for a respite from their kennel. Or maybe you could just sit with one and give it all the pets. There are options and the joy you will see on their faces will make it worth your while, I promise.

As you saw from my story about Daisy above, please make sure you are willing and able before adopting a pet. They are a "lifetime of the pet" commitment, so make sure you have thought it through. Do you travel a lot? If so, do you have a reliable pet sitter to take over while you are gone or a kennel that you trust to care for your animals? Can you care for a large dog or an active puppy? To thine own self be true. Don't get in over your head only to surrender your animal to a shelter or another owner. It doesn't always work out even with all good things but you want to give your new family member a wonderful "furever" home if possible.

Whichever way you go, you will be giving and receiving so much love!

1. So, think about your options. Are you ready for a dog? Research the different breeds to see which ones might be a good fit for you. Write them down and visit your local shelter to see if any might be available. Think about what supplies you may require in order to welcome them into your home and write those down as well. Normally, shelters don't require you to take the dog right away. You can put a hold on them and go back when you are ready. Good luck! I hope you find just the right companion if you don't already have one (or two+).

Notes:

Chapter Twenty-four

Have Faith in Your Life

Have faith in a Higher Power that has your back. Believe that you are not alone because you're not. Don't worry about stuff that you have no control over. Give it to your Higher Power and let "them" figure it out. Pray for others with all your heart. Wake up each day knowing you are loved.

How is your faith journey? There is a crisis in this country with organized religion. The traditional churches and other organized religions, are struggling. Were you raised with a belief from your family or have you found one on your own? No matter what "religion" you have, is it something you can rely on in your times of struggle? Does it give you a firm foundation for joy?

I was baptized in the Methodist church and my parents took me there regularly (I'm assuming). Then they fell off for some reason. When we moved to a new house and a new neighborhood, there was a church across the street, a Lutheran one. I felt compelled as a child to walk over there by myself to check it out. I began going to Sunday School on my own. Crazy right?

Then my girlfriend, Debbie who lived down the street informed me that she was going to go to her Grandma's church, a Presbyterian one this time, so that she might get confirmed. She invited me to go with her and I did, gladly. I think I was in 7th grade. We went through the process with other kids our age and my parents decided it might be time to get back to church upon my confirmation. We all became very active in this little church and I was so happy. But then the church struggled deeply and closed. That was the end of my church affiliation with my parents and it saddened me greatly.

My first job was as a church secretary at a big Presbyterian church. I began going on Sundays and joined the choir. There was so much history in that beautiful church and I felt a true connection there. I got married by one of their pastors, twice and stayed there until I faded away during my second marriage.

Once my children were teenagers, my sister, Lisa convinced me it was time to get back to church and Robin and I joined the Presbyterian church where she was a member. We went regularly, my children were confirmed and I became an elder and the clerk of the session. We loved this church as well, but when Robin and I moved an hour away, we also moved our membership to the small Presbyterian church in our new town. We joined it and this time, Robin became an elder but again, it faded into oblivion and closed when the membership became too small to support it.

My last church is a Wesleyan one which is just down the road from where I live now. It is a loving and welcoming church and I love the members. I struggle with some of their beliefs around homosexuality and abortion. Is it fair that I attend knowing I don't believe I am here to judge others around those issues (or any other for that matter)? I have been struggling with this more and more but I continue to attend and learn. What is the right way to practice your faith? You may have had a similar journey to mine with multiple churches and organized religions. I have learned much over the years from these different faiths but I think I've felt closer to God, my Higher Power of choice, the most when I was attending Alanon meetings (a support group for families and friends of alcoholics). That is where I truly learned how much I was loved by my Higher Power as well as those around me!

The Serenity Prayer became my mantra, at least the beginning of it:

> **God, grant me the serenity**
> **To accept the things I cannot change,**
> **Courage to change the things I can,**
> **And the wisdom to know the difference.**

You might ask why this was so critical in my life and the answer is a simple one for a complex thought process. I trusted that God would take care of me, no matter what. And he always has. Worry was not something I was interested in dwelling on, and this was something that my mom and I disagreed on until her death. She always felt I was naïve about life and my future because she worried about everything and attempted to control our family and their future. She always felt she knew what was best for others but I soon realized, that by forcing her will on others, she also put herself in the position to be responsible for the outcome. That is not something that I was interested in doing to my children, my friends or anyone else. I believe that God gave us free will so that we might learn our own lessons and create our own futures, based on our passions. Rather than always playing it safe, I became open to new possibilities and believed that if it didn't work out, I would find something else. Unfortunately, I did not truly find this strength until I joined Alanon in my 30's and met others who believed in me as well. Once I did, my life took off. I raised some amazing young women to believe in themselves by following their dreams, knowing that whatever happened, everything would be okay and even amazing.

So here I am in the last phase of my life and still solid in the faith that God has my back. I give my love freely to others and strive to build them up as well. I pray deeply for others each night before I shut my eyes to sleep and when I hear of a need, I add them to my prayer list. When I see someone who could use a hug, I give it to them. When I see someone and think, my how I love her hair or something he or she just did, I let them know. I compliment more than I criticize. The toughest feat I have is being kind to myself, but I am getting better. Knowing that I am loved by my Higher Power, my family and friends, and others I encounter, fills me with gratitude daily. I hope it does for you as well.

1. Think about your faith. How strong is it? How might you practice it? Take some time to really think about it. If you are not practicing at a traditional church every Sunday, that's okay. What does make you feel close to God or a Higher Power? Is it being in nature? Is it meditating? Is it reading the Bible, the Torah or the Koran? How about other spiritual books? What might you want to explore more deeply? Faith is a journey. Write down what your journey has been in the past and think about each of those chapters. When did you feel the closest to your Higher Power?

2. Now think about where you are today. Are you happy with your faith practice? What do you love about it? List it.

3. So where would you like to go in the future? Are there other avenues for you to explore? Would you like to spread the love you feel for yourself and others more frequently? Is there a church or other place of worship you would like to visit? Make a list of actions you'd like to take and get to it!

Notes:

Challenge

Wow! What an incredible journey you have been on thinking about retirement. Are you ready to take this next step in your career and your life? I can honestly tell you that I have enjoyed every day of mine, even the challenging ones. Here is your final task, for now.

1. I would love for you to start finalizing your decision on whether this is the right time for you to retire. List the concerns that you have that are preventing you from going for it below. Think about how you might overcome them and write it down next to each one. Are these reasons enough to keep you working?

2. Next, list the things you are most excited about doing once you retire. Is anything preventing you from doing them at this time? If so, can you overcome them?

3. Well, are you ready? If so, write down your goal date and get busy. You can do this! And remember, if you retire and are not happy with your new found freedom, you can always get another job. But give yourself time to settle into your new found freedom. It will take some getting used to! The first few weeks will feel like a vacation so it's usually after that time period that some people start to feel lost. If you are one of them, reread this book and see what you might be missing. Good luck and I wish you all the best in this phase of your life.

**I AM READY
AND THIS WILL BE MY
FINAL DAY OF WORK:**

Acknowledgements

I can't believe I did it! I would not have gotten this far without the love, guidance and support that I have received from so many people in my life.

Thank you to my husband, Robin, who has always been my biggest cheerleader, allowing me to lead and shine in whichever direction I chose to go. To my daughters, Jessie, De and Gill who have always believed in me even when I didn't believe in myself. To my dad, who always challenged me to be better and truly believed that I could be!

Thank you to my friend, Christine for giving me the perfect title for this book and to Kelly and Linda for reading my draft and providing the perfect edits and suggestions. Thank you to all my friends who have enriched my life in so many ways throughout the years.

Thank you to God for all the blessings he/she has bestowed on me throughout my life and for giving me the courage to try new things and the wherewithal to pick myself up when things didn't go as planned. I have always believed that he/she was watching over me and those I care about, and he/she always has!

About the author

Susan L. Klute went from stay-at-home mom to an award-winning sales executive and manager at the largest IT distributor in the world and an international manufacturer. In a career that spanned over 30 years, Susan mentored countless aspiring sales teams and guided and advocated for women around the world through her active leadership role in a global woman's network. In her retirement, she continues to inspire others through her art and writing. She lives in an 1800's farmhouse she renovated in the tiny hamlet of Appleton, NY with her husband Robin, their golden retriever, Daisy and their golden doodle, Delilah.

www.ingramcontent.com/pod-product-compliance
Lightning Source LLC
LaVergne TN
LVHW051834080426
835512LV00018B/2867